WITNESS

Witness

Book 2 of the Search for Truth Series

Ruth Chesney

JOHN RITCHIE LTD
CHRISTIAN PUBLICATIONS

40 Beansburn, Kilmarnock, Scotland

IF
Chesney

ISBN-13: 978 1 910513 62 0

Copyright © 2016 by John Ritchie Ltd.
40 Beansburn, Kilmarnock, Scotland

www.ritchiechristianmedia.co.uk

Unless otherwise indicated, Scripture quotations are taken from:
The Holy Bible, New King James Version®.
© 1982 by Thomas Nelson, Inc. Used by permission. All rights reserved.

Typeset by John Ritchie Ltd., Kilmarnock
Printed by Bell & Bain, Glasgow

For my parents,
John and Margaret Moore,
with heartfelt gratitude
for your love, care and godly example.

Acknowledgements

For the most part, writing a book is a solitary activity. However, when it comes to getting it ready for publication, a whole team of people is needed. I'm exceedingly thankful for those who give up their time to read the manuscript – finding errors, making suggestions and giving encouragement. To my mother, Margaret Moore, and my brother, Phillip Moore, many thanks for your honest yet uplifting critiques. To Eunice Wilkie, special thanks, not only for your help with this book, but for all the encouragement and support on my writing journey. To Joanne Grattan, thank you for your boundless, infectious enthusiasm, your desire to make this book as good as it can be and your very useful American input. Thanks to David and Jennie Williamson for your helpful comments and suggestions and for keeping this country girl right on all things Belfast! Special thanks to Jayne Ten for the detailed and invaluable answers to my many questions about Malaysian customs and religion, and for reading through the manuscript to eliminate the remaining errors. To Michael Wilkie, Michael Rodgers and Jason Miller, who assisted with the medical, police and fire scenes, and helped to give the book a flavour of authenticity, a big thank you. A teenage perspective is vital in writing a book such as this one, and so huge thanks again to Beth Herbison. I love reading your feedback and you will never know how much you encourage me. God bless you! And to Samuel, my husband, who faithfully and carefully reads through and corrects each manuscript, who puts up with late and hastily thrown together dinners on evenings when inspiration strikes and when deadlines loom, and who is willing to share his life with a vast array of imaginary people, thank you immensely for your patience, love and support.

Thanks once again to Alison and the team at John Ritchie Ltd for all their help, and to Pete Barnsley from Creative Hoot for another fantastic cover.

And to you, the reader. There would be no need to write books if no one wanted to read them, so thank you sincerely for taking the time. I trust and pray that you will be blessed by what you read – that if you aren't saved, you will soon come to know the Lord Jesus Christ as your Saviour, and if you are, that you will be encouraged to live for Him.

'Remember now your Creator in the days of your youth.'
Ecclesiastes 12:1

Prologue

"How dare you defy me?" the voice snarled venomously. "I will find you and you will pay, both you and that no-good Bible-bashing brat! Just you wait..."

Seb Mitchelson's eyes widened and he looked across at Mum. Her hand trembled as she ended the hateful flow of words spewing from the voice message. She didn't need to ask Seb if he had heard.

"That's not the first one," she told him, her face white. "I've blocked his number, but he keeps calling from different phones and leaving voicemails."

Seb shuddered and glanced out the window of the train at sheep grazing in green fields. The very sound of that voice caused unpleasant sensations to reawaken deep inside – a mixture of fear, worthlessness and weakness. He took a deep breath.

Mum gave him a shaky smile and slipped the phone back into her handbag resting on the grey plastic table between them. "It's okay," she said. "He won't find us. I don't think he'll even try. He's all noise." She bit her lip, looking unsure. "Still, it would do no harm to change my number. And, Seb, please be careful. Keep your eyes open."

Seb nodded. They both knew, no matter how much they wanted to believe otherwise, that the growling wasn't a harmless show of strength. Instead, it was a sign he was primed for attack – provoked, incensed and ready to strike.

They were familiar with this beast. They had been his victims before.

But never before had the anger been so intense. Never before had his authority been toppled so completely and his opinions disregarded so soundly as when Mum packed up her belongings and left him and when Seb threw his influence aside and became a Christian.

They needed to be on their guard, for this time his rage would know no bounds.

Chapter One

The deceleration of the train, coupled with the ever-widening tangle of railway lines outside and the sight of large, grey, metal sheds, caused a flurry of movement inside the train. People sprang to their feet, retrieved their bags from under seats and from the overhead storage racks, then jammed the aisles in the race to be first out the door. The train's brakes hissed and metal screeched against metal as the train finally slid to a stop. Doors beeped and glided open to disgorge the passengers onto Platform 2.

The red-bearded man opposite stood up, nodding in time to the beat pumping into his head from his earphones. He stuffed his arms into his navy duffle coat and shoved his iPhone into the pocket, earphones still embedded in his ears.

Mum smiled at Seb, a look of guarded excitement in her blue eyes. "Almost home," she said. Seb glanced over his shoulder to make sure the aisle was clear before standing and pulling his bag from the overhead storage rack. Mum dragged a large shopping bag from under the seat and pulled it into the aisle.

"Whew," she exclaimed. "It was so good of Karen to give me all this stuff, but now we've got to walk home with it."

"How far do we have to go?" asked Seb, as he stepped off the train and turned to wait for Mum.

"About twenty minutes' walk," she replied. "Not too far."

Seb took the bag from Mum. His arm dropped with the unexpected weight. "What's in here?" he asked.

"Oh, just some clothes, a pair of curtains Karen didn't need, and a few books."

Seb opened the bag and peered in. A round cake tin lay on top. "And this?" He pointed at the box.

"That's a fruitcake Karen made. She found Granny's old recipe for Christmas cake earlier this year and wanted me to taste it to see if she's got it right. She remembered that I always loved Christmas cake when I was a child." She smiled wistfully.

"Really?" he asked. "I've never seen Christmas cake in our house."

Mum shook her head sadly. "I stopped buying Christmas cake years ago. Your dad hates dried fruit, so there wasn't much point in buying one just for me."

His mum loved Christmas cake? Why had he never known that before? Seb had a sudden suspicion that there was a lot more about her and her childhood that he didn't know. *Things will be different now*, he thought. Now that his mum had a new house, and it would just be the two of them, there would be lots of time for Seb to find out things about her that he'd never been interested in prior to his trip to Cherryhill Farm. Before he left Belfast at the beginning of the summer, he'd never thought about Mum's childhood. Aunt Karen, who was Mum's sister, her husband, Matt, and daughters, Lavinia and Martha, were only names to him. But they had become very special to Seb, closer family than even his own dad, who Seb now realised didn't act much like a father at all. He especially wanted to know why Mum felt that it was too late for her to be saved. What had she done that she felt was so unforgiveable?

Mum lifted the heavy bag from Seb and hoisted it onto her arm. "This way," she said, pointing towards the exit.

They had barely left the front doors of the train station when Mum started to slow. Grimacing, she lifted the bag to her other arm.

"Here, Mum," said Seb. "Why don't you take my bag instead? It's not much lighter, but you can carry it over your shoulder."

Mum smiled gratefully at him as she handed over the bag and turned left onto a road, busy with Tuesday evening rush hour traffic. "You likely can manage to carry it better than I can anyway. All that fresh air and hard work on the farm. You've grown at least a couple of inches too, I think."

"That's likely because of Aunt Karen's– " Seb quickly stopped.

"Good cooking?" finished Mum.

Seb nodded sheepishly. "I don't mean that your cooking is bad, but Aunt Karen always had really big meals and she made everything from scratch…" He trailed off, aware that the more he said, the worse it sounded.

Mum laughed. "It's okay, Seb," she said. "I know you didn't get great meals at home before, but things are going to be different now. There won't be much money left over after I pay the rent, but we'll have enough to eat healthily. At least I know that it won't have disappeared when I go to look for it."

Seb knew what she meant. Dad's drinking habit had wreaked havoc on the family's finances; and not only the finances, but on the atmosphere in their home. Dad was a violent drunk and Mum bore more than a few scars as a result of his drunken rages.

———

The new house was located halfway down a quiet street lined with two identical rows of small, red-brick houses. The doors opened directly onto the street. Mum stopped outside a brown door and pulled a key from her black handbag. Turning the key in the lock, she pushed the door open and stood back.

"Welcome home, Seb," she said, smiling, as she gestured for him to step in first.

Seb took a step into the little house. The stairs were directly ahead and there was a frosted glass door to the right. He opened it and stepped into a living room. The walls were painted cream and the sofa and armchair were covered with bright pink throw blankets. A small table and two chairs sat against the opposite wall, beside a door leading to what Seb presumed must be the kitchen. "Come upstairs and I'll show you your bedroom," said Mum, biting her lip a little nervously.

Seb followed her upstairs.

"Bathroom is here," Mum said, pushing open the door at the head of the stairs. She opened the door to the room beside the bathroom. "This is your room."

Seb stepped into a small, dark room. He dumped his bag on the single bed which was pushed against the wall. A wardrobe stood against the wall to his right, almost behind the door.

"I haven't decorated it yet," Mum said. "I thought I would ask you first what colour scheme you'd like."

Seb shrugged. He didn't really mind. He moved to the window and looked out. The houses of another street backed up to the houses of his street. If it hadn't been for the net curtains hanging at the windows of the other house, he could have almost seen right into the house. Directly under his window was a small, empty back yard with a washing line. The back yard next door caught his eye. Crammed full of pots and plants of every description, it was a bright spot of colour in an otherwise drab scene.

"Who lives there?" he asked Mum.

"Oh, that's Mrs Thompson," she said. "Aren't her flowers beautiful? She's offered to give me a few to brighten up our yard too."

Seb turned away from the window and followed Mum out the door as she showed him her bedroom at the front of the house. The house was small. Even smaller than the last house they'd lived in, and tiny compared to the farmhouse at Cherryhill. But this was now home. There were no bad memories here. Mum had gone to a great deal of effort and it was clean and tidy. It smelled good too, no lingering tobacco or alcohol smells. And, best of all, it was peaceful.

"Seb, dinner!" called Mum, a short while later. Seb got off the bed and went downstairs to find two plates of pasta in a tomato sauce on the table.

"I'm sorry it isn't very much," she said, "and certainly not as good as the food Karen would have given you."

"It smells good." Seb pulled out his chair and sat down.

Mum went to lift her fork, then paused.

Seb looked at her inquisitively. "What is it?"

"Oh, nothing," she said. "I just wondered if you'd want to give thanks for the food."

Seb swallowed. He prayed plenty on his own, but he'd never yet prayed audibly in front of anyone. He'd planned on saying a silent prayer of thanks. And yet, his mum wasn't a believer. If she expected him to pray...

"Okay," he said, closing his eyes. "God, we want to give thanks for this food, in the name of our Lord Jesus Christ. Amen." He opened his eyes and glanced at his mum. She lifted her fork and smiled at him.

"Short and sweet. No point in big long prayers when the food's on the table. We don't want it getting cold." She ate a forkful of pasta. "We have lots to do tomorrow. There's no way last year's school uniform will fit you, so we'll need to go and buy you new clothes, and I'd like to get paint for your room."

"Can we afford all that?" Seb asked.

"Well, just about," replied Mum. "The curtains Karen gave me will save me having to buy any for my bedroom."

"I don't mind if I don't get my bedroom decorated yet."

Mum's eyes filled with tears and she gave Seb a watery smile. "Are you sure?" she asked.

Seb nodded. "It's fine the way it is."

Mum reached across and squeezed his arm. "Thank you, Seb." She looked quite relieved, but Seb could still detect a troubled look in her blue eyes. No wonder, she had plenty of worries these days. He'd have to pray a lot more earnestly for her salvation. While it wouldn't remove her problems, having the Lord Jesus Christ as her Saviour and Friend would certainly help her to cope much better.

———

Seb yawned and stretched. *Thump.* His elbow banged against something solid. He rubbed it and opened his eyes a crack. A wall? Sunlight was streaming through the thin curtains. He gazed around the room, confused. Gradually his memory awakened. Belfast. Mum's house. He'd left Cherryhill yesterday and was now back in the city. School was starting tomorrow and today they were going to get his uniform. He could hear running water and the hum of the fan in the bathroom next door.

Swinging his legs out of bed, he pulled back the edge of the curtain and looked out. Houses and yards, stretching in neat lines. He sighed. He missed the green fields and tall trees, the lowing of the cows and the singing of the birds, the fresh air... *and farm smells,* he thought, smiling wryly. They beat traffic fumes any day.

"How did you sleep?" asked Mum at breakfast time.

"It took me a while to drop over," he said, buttering his toast. "I'd forgotten how noisy it is in Belfast."

Mum nodded, her eyes glazing over with the memory of a long-ago scene. "I remember when I first came to live in Belfast," she said. "I couldn't sleep with the streetlight outside my window. I ended up taping a sheet of cardboard to the window every night." She laughed drily. "After a while, I got used to it... " She drifted off, a look of sadness in her eyes.

Seb watched his mum. He guessed she wasn't just talking about the streetlights. What was her story?

Mum shook her head and blinked, then pasted a smile on her face. "Well," she said brightly, "a bus passes the end of the street just after ten. I hope I brought everything you need for school from the last house. I cleared out all I could, but I'm sure I've forgotten something. The house was in such a mess."

Seb nodded. He was sure it would be in an even bigger mess now with just his dad living there and no one to clean up after him. Or was he still there? Could Dad even afford the rent?

"I put your things in the wardrobe, and there are some more bags in the cupboard under the stairs. Sort through everything and see what you need. We'll leave as soon as you're ready."

———

The bus pulled to a halt and Seb stepped down onto the street, arms laden with bags. Mum followed, her arms full as well. They'd had a successful trip – Seb had got his uniform and new school supplies. Mum had even found some half-price bedlinen for Seb's room, and a reduced-price damaged tin of paint.

"The next day I'm off work I'll try to paint your room," Mum said later as she stored the tin of paint under the stairs. "I'm sorry it's not the shade of blue you wanted, though."

"It's okay," he replied. "I don't really mind."

Mum gave her head a little shake and looked at him in amazement. "You've changed so much, Seb," she said, putting an arm around his shoulders.

Seb smiled. He really had. But – his smile faded – school started in the morning and the new Seb wasn't going to be very popular there anymore. It wasn't just because he had discovered an interest in agriculture; he knew that becoming a Christian was going to lead to a lot of problems. It was so much easier at Cherryhill, where there were lots of other Christians around, but now he'd have to take a stand for Christ in an opposing and unsympathetic world. What would Tyler say? His other friends? He bit his lip. Mr Symons, his biology teacher, who made no pretence of the fact that he believed that God was a myth. His stomach clenched and he suddenly felt very alone. He didn't know one other Christian in the city. No doubt there were others, but he didn't know where they might be.

I am with you always...

Seb took a deep breath as the words he'd read in his Bible, spoken by the Lord Jesus Christ after His resurrection, filled his soul with peace. No matter what happened, whether he was ostracised, ridiculed or scorned, he was never alone. Not when Christ was with him as He had promised. He grasped the promise tightly. He would need it.

Chapter Two

The corridors buzzed with a nervous first day of school energy as Seb walked towards his allocated form room on Thursday morning. It was all so familiar, and yet he felt as if he had stepped into another world. Almost as if he had ceased to belong here, among these people and in this environment.

"Hey, Seb!" Tyler called from the area of the lockers.

Seb turned around. "Hi, Tyler! Hi, Corey!" He walked over to join the boys. Tyler and Corey had been his closest friends before the summer. In fact, Seb had complained bitterly to them when he'd found out he was going to be packed off to Cherryhill Farm.

"We haven't seen you all summer. Were you really on a farm the whole time?" Corey asked.

Seb smiled. "Pretty much. It was good, though."

Tyler and Corey looked at each other incredulously.

"Did you drive tractors and milk cows?" Tyler scoffed.

"Yes," Seb replied.

Tyler looked at him for an instant before bursting into laughter. "Ha-ha! Good one, Seb! You really had me convinced for a minute."

Seb shrugged. "It's true. I helped out. And I helped stop cattle rustlers–"

"Hold on a minute, Seb," interrupted Corey. "You don't need to make stuff up. What crazy story will you tell us next?"

Seb bit his lip. There actually was something else that his friends would find even less believable than the thought of Seb milking cows. "Um…"

The bell rang loud and shrill, drowning out what Seb had been about to say.

"Right, people, get to your form rooms," Mr Harding shouted. "You can't hang around here all day."

Seb hefted his school bag on to his shoulder and followed the boys to registration. He felt sick. He had missed an opportunity to tell them that he was now a believer in the Lord Jesus Christ. And yet he felt oddly relieved that he could hide a little longer. He could only imagine what they might say.

On arrival at the classroom, the boys grabbed their usual seats at the back. The noise was deafening, with shouts and calls. Tyler began to blow tiny wads of soggy paper through an empty pen at Madison, which got caught in her long blonde hair. "Yuck, Tyler, that's disgusting," she exclaimed as she picked them out and flung them on the floor.

"*Yuck, Tyler, that's disgusting,*" he mocked in a shrill voice. "Hey, look." He pointed at the front of the classroom. "A new boy!" He pulled an elastic band from his pocket and aimed a folded paper missile at the back of the black-haired head.

Ping! The paper bullet hit its target and ricocheted. The boy jumped and lifted a hand to rub his head before turning around to determine the source of the attack.

"Oh, look!" Tyler nudged Seb, eyes widening as he took in the straight black hair and Asian features. He shouted a derogatory name at the boy. The rest of the class looked to see who Tyler was yelling at, and began to laugh. The boy turned back around and stared intently at the whiteboard, shoulders squared.

"Tyler, stop that," said Seb intently, in a quiet voice.

Tyler stopped shouting and gave Seb a puzzled look. "What's got into you?" he asked. "Has living on a farm turned you into a goody-goody?"

Seb shook his head and took a deep breath. "No, but over the summer I became–"

"Right, class!" boomed a voice from the doorway. "Far too much noise on the first day. Settle down or you'll all be in detention." Mr Symons, his form teacher, strode into the room.

Everyone sat up a little straighter and the yelling subsided. Seb sighed. He would have to wait until another time.

———

Seb glanced around the crowded canteen, then lifted his tray and weaved his way to their favourite table in the far corner of the room. Madison and her friend Zoe were already there. As Seb set down his tray, he heard a crash of a plate and cutlery hitting the floor. The room erupted in a cheer. Tyler was standing, bent over in laughter, beside a boy sprawled on the floor, rice and curry strewn around him. Seb's face tightened in anger as he recognised the new boy. He could hear Madison and Zoe giggle behind him as Tyler swaggered over, a silly smile on his face. Seb spun around to look at the girls.

"What are you laughing at?" he demanded. They blinked at him, confused, their giggles momentarily stilled. Seb didn't wait for an answer. He turned to Tyler. "What did you do that for?"

Tyler sniggered. "Do what?"

"You know what you did! You tripped him up!"

Tyler laughed. "He wasn't looking where he was going." He looked quizzically at Seb. "But why are you getting so annoyed about it? He's only a foreigner; he deserves it!"

Seb took a step closer. "He does *not* deserve it," he hissed. "He's done nothing wrong and I don't know why you're picking on him."

Tyler's mouth fell open. "I didn't think you had a problem with having a bit of fun. Don't you remember the way you use to wind up Pawel?"

Seb sank into his seat. Tyler was right. He had done a lot worse to the Polish boy in his class last year. Pawel had finally changed schools. "Sit down, Tyler, I want to tell you something."

Tyler looked suspiciously at him and sat down. "What is it?" he asked. Madison and Zoe had lost interest in their lunches and were staring intently, waiting to hear what Seb had to say.

Corey chose that moment to join them with his tray. "Hey, mate, what happened over there?" He slid into the seat and pointed in the direction of the new boy, where the cleaners were busy cleaning up the spilled rice.

"Shush," said Tyler. "Seb has something *very important* to tell us." He wiggled his eyebrows.

Seb took a deep breath. It was now or never. He sent up a silent plea for help. He could feel his legs trembling. *I can do all things through Christ who strengthens me*, flooded through his soul. He cleared his throat. "You know the way I was at the farm this summer?"

"Oh, yes, milking cows and driving tractors," laughed Corey. "Have you decided to be a farmer when you leave this dump?"

"Maybe," Seb began, "but..."

"Oh, he *is* going to be a farmer. Farmer Seb! Ha-ha!" laughed Tyler.

"Oo ar!" mocked Corey.

"Tyler! Corey!" Seb was getting exasperated. He was determined to tell them this time. "That's not what I was going to tell you. I wanted to tell you that when I was at the farm I got saved."

Tyler scrunched up his nose and looked at Seb. "You what? Got saved? What's that?"

"It means I became a Christian," replied Seb.

Tyler and Corey erupted in laughter. He didn't look round but he could hear the girls' giggles. "Oh, that's brilliant, Seb! The best joke I've ever heard," chortled Tyler.

Seb shook his head. "But, Tyler, it's true! Honestly!"

Tyler's laughter fizzled out. "True? You're a Christian?"

Seb nodded.

"But you were an atheist before the summer."

"Yes."

Corey leaned back in his seat. "You've been brainwashed, mate. Those stupid farmers that you lived with, they've no brains and don't know any better. Sure everybody knows there's no God."

"But there *is* a God," replied Seb. "How do you think everything came into existence?"

"Uh, the Big Bang! Duh!"

"So if there was a big bang, what made it happen? And how did something come from nothing?"

Corey shrugged. "It just did. Why don't you ask Miss Carruthers?"

Seb glanced at Madison and Zoe. Madison looked puzzled and Zoe was focussed on picking at her bright pink nail polish.

"And anyway," he continued, "a Christian isn't just someone who believes that there is a God. A Christian is someone who has trusted in the Lord Jesus Christ. He died on the cross to take away our sins–"

"Ugh, shut up, Seb," said Tyler. "I can't believe you've gone all religious. That explains why you're no fun anymore. Why can't you just forget about the whole religion business and be yourself again?"

"But I'm not the same person," Seb explained. " 'If anyone is in Christ, he is a new creation,' the Bible says."

Corey groaned. "Aw, no! He's rhyming the Bible at us now!"

Seb shook his head and ate a forkful of his pasta bake. There was no point in saying anything more right now: they obviously didn't want to hear it.

Seb stayed in the canteen after the others had left, and pulled his Bible from his bag. He opened it at Paul's letter to the Colossians where he'd left off reading that morning. A verse caught his eye. *That you may walk worthy of the Lord, fully pleasing Him, being fruitful in every good work and increasing in the knowledge of God...* He paused. That was quite a challenge in this environment, surrounded by foul language, obscene conversations and everything else that went on in his school.

Suddenly, the bell rang, signalling the end of lunchtime and making him jump. He placed the Bible back in his bag, exited the canteen and walked down the corridor. As Seb was putting a book into his locker, he caught the end of a conversation around the corner.

"I can't believe Seb is a Christian." It was Madison.

"He has changed *so much* since last year," came Zoe's reply. "I mean, he's got taller and he's so tanned..." She giggled.

"I think you fancy him!" replied Madison.

"Hey!"

"I wouldn't blame you."

The two girls laughed. Seb inwardly groaned and slammed the locker shut.

"But he's a Christian. Did you understand all this *saved* stuff he was talking about?" Madison asked.

"Uh, sort of," replied Zoe.

"Well, I haven't a clue," Madison declared. "Tyler and Corey weren't too impressed either!"

The voices grew closer and Seb quickly left the locker bay. He was glad he'd had an opportunity to tell his friends that he was now a believer and, despite their scoffing, he hoped that they could see the change in him.

———

Seb turned the key in the lock and pushed open the door. Mum was at work and the house was quiet. He dumped his school bag beside the table and went in search of some food. A plastic box lay on the bench. He shook it, then lifted the lid. The smell of fresh scones wafted towards him. He reached in and helped himself to a couple. Beside the kettle sat a pot of jam bearing a label which read *Raspberry Jam* in old-fashioned handwriting. Likely from Mrs Thompson – Mum had said she spent a lot of time in her kitchen and liked to give away most of what she made. He smiled as he found a plate and a knife and then liberally slathered butter and jam over each scone half. After grabbing a mug, he filled it with milk and carried his snack through to the table in the living room. Seb lifted his maths homework out of his bag and spread it out on the table. As he lifted his hand to reach for the scone, his phone rang. Pulling it out of his pocket, he glanced at the screen. He didn't recognise the number. Maybe someone he had met over the summer…?

The slurred voice was instantly recognisable. "Where a-a-are youuuuu, s-s-son?"

Dad! Seb grimaced. He wished he hadn't answered it.

"I'm at home," he said.

"Wh-wh-where's home?"

"I can't tell you that," Seb replied, after a pause.

"Wh-wh-why n-n-not?"

"Dad, you've been drinking," said Seb. "I'm busy. I have maths homework to do."

"W-w-wait! C-c-come back. Live here. Plenty of m-m-money now."

Seb frowned. Plenty of money? His dad never had money. Anything he earned, he spent on alcohol.

"Dad, you're drunk. And I really need to go. Bye!" Seb ended the call and turned the phone off before Dad could call back. Leaning back in his seat, he turned the phone over in his hands. What on earth had Dad been talking about? Maybe he thought that Mum had plenty of money now and he wanted to get his hands on it. Seb nodded. Yes, that was probably what he meant. He was likely struggling now that Mum wasn't around to fund him anymore. Seb set down the phone and lifted the scone.

By the time Mum came home from work, the box of scones was almost depleted, and the homework was done.

"I don't remember you doing homework since you were at primary school," she said in surprise.

Seb smiled. "I never did any."

Mum shook her head. "I know! The teachers kept telling me, but what could I do? You wouldn't listen to me. I just can't get over the difference in you."

"God's salvation, Mum," he called, as he ran upstairs to change out of his uniform. "It could change you too!"

Chapter Three

"Okay, class!" diminutive Mrs Jones shouted at the top of her voice. The din continued, so she banged the side of a heavy textbook on her desk. The noise subsided a little. "That's better. Now," she continued, peering around the room, her hands twitching by her sides, "who did their homework last night?"

Two hands rose. Mrs Jones smiled at the new boy at the front of the room, then her gaze flitted around and came to rest on Seb. She frowned. "You did, Seb?" she asked, puzzled.

Seb nodded and held out his book for her inspection.

Mrs Jones grabbed her reading glasses, perched them on the end of her nose and trotted down the room to examine Seb's homework. She gave her head a little shake, whipped the glasses off and rubbed her eyes. She spun around to face the board and back again to Seb's homework. Leaning down, she rested her hands on the desk in front of Seb and spoke quietly. "Did you do this yourself?"

Seb nodded. "Yes, Mrs Jones."

Again she shook her head and went back to her desk. "Well." She opened a drawer and closed it again, then snatched up a pen. "Let's go through the answers. Open your books, class," she said, gesturing with her pen. As she did so, the pen flew from her fingers and through the open window. She gazed after it in shock. "My pen!" she exclaimed, rushing to the window and staring down at the ground three storeys below.

The room erupted in laughter.

"Will I go and find it, Mrs Jones?" shouted Tyler.

Mrs Jones straightened herself up and cleared her throat. "No, Tyler, it's fine. I have another pen here..." She fumbled around her desk, lifting papers and pushing books aside. "...Somewhere...I'm certain...Aha!" She pulled another pen from inside the textbook and held it up with a flourish. "Now," she continued, "question one. What is the answer?"

The new boy raised his hand.

"Yes?"

"10."

"Excellent!" Mrs Jones beamed. "Did anyone else get that right?"

Seb looked down at his book. 14. He sighed. It was one thing doing homework, but another thing entirely actually getting it right

"Okay, let's work through this together. Our formula is $a^2 + b^2 = c^2$. If 'a' is 8 and 'b' is 6..."

The bell rang. Seb closed his books and shoved them into his bag

He had got only one question right. He didn't know what he was doing wrong, but he had a sneaking suspicion that it had something to do with the fact that he wasn't at the level he should be. Maths had never mattered to him before; his only ambition had been to leave school as soon as possible. His summer at Cherryhill had changed all that. Now the last thing he wanted was to waste his life.

Seb hoisted his bag onto his shoulder and made his way out of the room. Turning left down the corridor, he walked towards Mr Symons' classroom. This was the first class with his atheistic biology teacher since he had got saved and he felt a little nervous. Mr Symons liked to talk about the folly of people who believe in creation, but Seb hoped that, today being the first class of this school year, he would get a reprieve.

"Right, class, good to see you all back here and ready to work," Mr Symons said sarcastically as he smirked at the roomful of restless teenagers. "I hope you all had a good summer. I can't imagine that any of you did anything terribly exciting. Stuff you shouldn't have done, most likely. Illegal things...?" He gazed around the room, eyebrows raised, lip curled.

Tyler and Corey looked at each other and laughed. Seb knew that they had planned to experiment with drugs this summer and he would have been in the middle of it had he not been sent to the farm. At the time he was angry that he was missing out, but now he was more than thankful.

"Care to share with the rest of us what you did this summer?" Mr Symons had stopped beside Corey's desk and was frowning down at him. "Something I said seemed to resonate with you and Tyler."

Corey looked up at him, a blank look on his face.

Mr Symons gave a short laugh. "Resonate – look it up. You lot need to extend your vocabulary. So what was it that you and Tyler were laughing at?"

"Uh, nothing," replied Corey nonchalantly.

"Tyler?" Mr Symons called.

"Nothing much, Mr Symons," Tyler said, shrugging, then a wicked gleam came into his eye. "But Seb had an interesting summer."

Mr Symons' attention switched focus and lighted on Seb. "Well, enlighten us, Seb, as to your interesting summer." He had a half smile on his face. Seb wondered what he was expecting him to say.

"I went to stay with my uncle and aunt on a farm," he replied.

Mr Symons' eyes widened in surprise. "Well, Seb! That is something different. Did you help out on the farm?"

Seb nodded. "I helped with milking, clearing out calf pens and bringing in the silage."

A ripple of laughter spread through the class at Seb's words.

Mr Symons looked around the room. "Don't laugh, class," he said. "I'm impressed! Seb's knowledge will come in very useful this year. Now, you'll see I've left textbooks on every desk. Open them up to the first chapter."

Seb opened his book, then glanced across the classroom. Tyler was mouthing something at Corey, who was struggling to control his laughter.

Mr Symons had also spotted the two boys. "Corey! Tyler!" he exclaimed. "What is it now?"

Tyler grinned, then shot a triumphant look in Seb's direction. Seb frowned. What was going on?

"We were just wondering what you'd think about Seb becoming a Christian."

The class seemed to collectively gasp, and every head turned to gauge Mr Symons' reaction. Seb braced himself.

Mr Symons strolled down the classroom, a sardonic smile on his face. "So, Seb," he said drily, "the ignorant farmers were persuasive, were they?"

"Mr Symons, my uncle is a very intelligent man. He's not ignorant!"

"As far as science is concerned, it sounds like he's very ignorant."

"He has a degree in agricultural science!"

"Huh! Hardly the same thing," he muttered, before spinning on his heels and marching to his desk. "Well, Seb, you'll enjoy one of the topics we're covering this year – evolution and natural selection." He made a noise Seb could only describe as a cackle.

Seb was dismayed. He knew Mr Symons well enough to know that he would make Seb an object lesson on gullibility. Still, he reminded himself, Mr Symons wasn't the final authority. He was only one small man on a tiny planet in a vast universe, vainly shaking his fist against the Creator of everything.

———

After Seb had eaten his lunch, he again pulled out his Bible. Tyler and Corey had eaten with him, but had since left. Seb wasn't sure where they had gone, maybe out behind the bicycle sheds for a smoke or something. He had barely opened the book when Andrew from the year below poked his head into the canteen. "Hey, you guys really want to see this," he called, then dashed back in the direction he'd come from.

Suddenly the room cleared as everyone ran to see what was going on. Seb had a sinking feeling; whatever was happening, he knew it couldn't be good. He pushed the Bible back into his bag and sped after everyone else.

The crowd seemed to be spilling out the door to the boys' toilets. Seb pushed his way forward. "What's going on?" he asked. The screams of someone inside one of the cubicles was almost drowned out by the laughter of those standing nearby. He thought he detected Tyler's distinctive high-pitched screeching laughter. Seb was filled with dread. With a strength born of desperation, he forced his way through the crowd, standing on toes and elbowing ribs, in his attempt to reach the centre of everyone's attention. When he did finally make it to the toilet cubicle, what he saw made his blood boil.

Tyler and Corey were standing on either side of someone who was bending low over the toilet. So low, in fact, that his head was below the rim of the toilet bowl. Corey chose that moment to press the flusher and the boys pushed the head further into the toilet.

Seb saw red. With a growl, he sprang forward and grabbed Tyler, who happened to be closest. He hauled him out of the cubicle and slammed him against the wall. Tyler froze in shock, and before he could move, Seb had driven a fist hard into his nose. "How dare you do that?" he screamed, drawing back his arm for another blow. Tyler had raised his arm in front of his face, blood streaming from his nose onto his white shirt. As Seb drove his arm forward, it was suddenly jolted to a stop.

"Right, Mitchelson," Mr Symons' voice broke into his consciousness. "What is the meaning of this?"

Seb felt his shoulders slump. What had he just done?! And of all the teachers in the school to appear...

"I'm sorry, Mr Symons," he said, turning around and scuffing at the ground with his toe.

"I think you should say that to Tyler instead! What in the world made you do that?"

Seb lifted his head and glanced around. Corey was standing just behind Mr Symons, eyes wide. Inside the toilet cubicle was the new boy, looking stunned and shaken, black hair dripping, face pale. Seb had correctly guessed the victim. He pointed at the boy.

Mr Symons looked at him and back at Seb. "What about him?" he asked.

"He was having his head flushed down the toilet."

Mr Symons gave a mirthless laugh. "So that's what it's all about. Seb the Christian tries to save the day! Well, let me tell you, Seb, that you're just doing what has been done for years – using religion as an excuse to fight."

Seb gritted his teeth and inwardly groaned. The dawning realisation of what he'd done was making him feel sick. What a start to his Christian witness at school. He'd failed. He'd let God down in front of his friends, schoolmates and, worst of all, Mr Symons.

Mr Symons shook his head and turned around. "Right, you lot," he yelled at the crowd, "clear off! Corey, make yourself useful and grab some toilet roll for Tyler before he bleeds over everything, then get him to the nurse. You," he pointed at the new boy, "may go home and get yourself cleaned up. And Seb, you're coming with me. I think Ms Armstrong will want a word."

Seb grimaced. He'd been in the principal's office many times over his few short years at this school, but he really had thought those days were over. He glanced back at Tyler as he left the toilets. Tyler was sitting on the floor, his back against the wall, with a wad of rapidly reddening toilet roll held at his nose.

Sorry, Seb mouthed at him. He narrowed his eyes and glared at Seb.

Ms Armstrong shook her spiky platinum-blonde head as Mr Symons and Seb walked into the room. "Well. What is it this time?" she asked.

"I found Seb picking a fight with Tyler Hutchins in the toilets," replied Mr Symons.

Seb's head jerked around to look at his biology teacher. He was deliberately misleading Ms Armstrong!

"And why did you feel the need to do this?" Ms Armstrong intoned, pulling off her tortoiseshell spectacles.

"I found Tyler and Corey in the toilets, pushing the–" Seb began.

"Oh, do you know what?" Ms Armstrong waved her hand. "I have enough on my plate right now. I don't really have time to listen to your excuses. This is the second day of school and you're in trouble again already. I'm sure Mr Symons can arrange an appropriate punishment."

Mr Symons nodded slowly and scratched his beard. A half smile emerged on his face. "Yes, Ms Armstrong, I can deal with this."

"Well, good!" She turned her attention back to the computer screen. "But, Seb, the next time I hear that you're in trouble, there'll be greater consequences. Okay?"

"Yes, Ms Armstrong," Seb replied. In one sense he was relieved that she hadn't phoned Mum, but he was angry that Tyler and

Corey were going to get away with their racist bullying. Mr Symons obviously didn't care.

Mr Symons pushed open the door to his classroom and motioned for Seb to follow. He pulled a slip of paper from his desk and handed it to Seb. "After-school detention on Monday. This is a huge mark against you so early in the school year. Now go, and try to keep out of trouble for once."

Seb turned and walked out of the room, closing the door behind him. He couldn't believe it. Things were supposed to be so different this year, and instead he had ended up getting detention on his second day. He walked down the corridor, downcast and confused. How had he ended up failing so badly?

Chapter Four

For the Friday afternoon English class, time dragged, but Mr Kerry's voice droning in the background and the unsettled movements and chatter of his fellow pupils never penetrated Seb's bubble. For him, it seemed as if time had stopped completely and the world only consisted of him and his guilt. He couldn't believe he had lost his temper so badly. What Tyler and Corey had been doing was wrong; there was no question of that, but for Seb to do what he did…! Christians were supposed to be like Christ, and punching someone in the nose was certainly far from ideal Christian behaviour. In fact – Seb's heart sank further as a sudden realisation struck him – it was like something his dad would do. He almost groaned out loud. His dad was the last person he wanted to be like.

The bell rang and Mr Kerry wrapped up the lesson. The rest of the class made a beeline for the door and Seb pushed his books into his bag. As he stood up, a sudden thought struck his mind with horror and despair and he grabbed the chair-back to steady himself. Christians couldn't sin like that, could they? Maybe he wasn't actually a Christian after all!

———

Seb made his way out of the school gate and turned left towards home. The events of the day played and replayed themselves over in his mind. When he reached the moment where he realised what Tyler and Corey were doing, he wished he could press *stop* and do something differently – run for a teacher, pull the new boy out of danger – anything but drive his fist into Tyler's nose. But Seb watched in horror as again and again he saw himself losing control. *What must God think?* he agonised.

He turned left again at the end of the road and took a shortcut through a piece of wasteland. An old building had been knocked down and the site cleared, but the developers had never returned to build. As he walked across the rough ground, he became aware of voices behind him. He quickened his pace. Although he didn't have far to go, right now he was hidden from the view of either road.

Footsteps sounded behind him. Faster and faster they came. Seb began to sprint. He was at a distinct disadvantage, beginning to run from a slow walking speed, while carrying a heavy schoolbag of books. He took a quick glance behind him but could only see someone wearing a black sweatshirt, hood up. At that moment, his foot caught on the uneven surface and he stumbled. As he struggled to regain his balance, someone grabbed his arm from behind and spun him around.

"You little creep!" It was Tyler's older brother, Lee. He gave Seb a shake. "Let's see how tough you are now!" He let go and put up both fists, dancing from one foot to the other.

"Lee," began Seb.

"What is it? Too scared? Or want to fight with something else?" A mean look came into his eyes and he drew out a small knife from the pocket of his baggy trousers.

"Please, Lee, I didn't mean to hit Tyler. I just got mad. I don't want to fight."

Lee began to jab the blade at Seb. Seb clenched his fists by his sides, trying to control their wild trembling. He wished that Lee would just go away.

Suddenly, Lee reached out and grabbed his arm. Seb took a deep breath and waited for the sharp pain. Instead he heard the tearing of fabric and his arm was suddenly released.

"I'll let you off this time," said Lee with a sneer. "But see next time..." He turned on his heel and left. As he joined his companions, Seb could hear them say, "Hey, did you see the look on his face? That was priceless!"

Seb picked up his bag. The sleeve of his brand-new school blazer flopped open, cut from wrist to elbow. He winced. Now he was going to have to explain everything to Mum. He wondered how much worse today could get.

———

As he turned the key in the lock, he heard a cheery voice from next door. "Hello, young man. You must be Seb."

Seb paused. Of all the days to meet his new neighbour, it had to be today. He arranged his face into a smile and turned around. "Mrs Thompson."

The white-haired lady reached out to shake hands with Seb and her eyes widened when she saw his sleeve. "My dear boy," she said. "What happened?"

Seb shook his head. "It's a long story."

"Well, I've a freshly-baked Victoria sponge, a newly-brewed pot of tea and plenty of time. Come on." She put her hand on his shoulder and, when he had relocked the door, ushered him into her little house.

"Take a seat and I'll get you some cake." Mrs Thompson waved him towards the sofa before stepping into the kitchen. Seb dumped his schoolbag on the floor and gingerly pushed a couple of crocheted cushions out of the way to make room to sit down.

Mrs Thompson's house was the same layout as Seb's, but instead of painted walls, it had bright flowered wallpaper. Family pictures lined the walls and various ornaments and figurines rested on the mantelpiece, windowsill and side table. A large wall clock ticked loudly. A ginger cat was curled up in an armchair beside the fireplace and Seb noted with interest that a Bible lay open on the table in the corner of the room. Could it be that this lady was saved?

The old lady reappeared with a tray stacked with two mugs of tea and two plates, large slices of sponge cake and a small fork on each. "I love baking," she told Seb, as she handed him a plate of cake, "but since Bobby died, I've no one to bake for. My son, Robert," she pointed to a framed picture of a young man in a graduation robe and cap, "lives in London. He's an architect. He's married and has two daughters. They come over occasionally, but they're all so busy." She smiled wistfully, then absently shooed the cat off the armchair and sat down. The cat yawned and stretched, then curled up on the hearthrug instead.

"So, Seb," Mrs Thompson said when the slices of cake had been eaten. "You said that you had a long story. Care to tell me?"

Seb sighed. He didn't really want to tell a perfect stranger about his day, but if she was a true believer in the Lord Jesus, as he hoped she might be, then she would be the only Christian he knew in the city of Belfast. Maybe she could help him.

Mrs Thompson smiled. "It's all right, Seb. I can see you'd rather not talk about it just yet. But how about I sew up that sleeve for you? Your mum is a busy lady and I'm quite certain she won't want to buy you a new jacket so soon."

Seb gave a faint smile. "You're right about that!" he said and slipped off the blazer.

Mrs Thompson stood up and crossed the room to a large cupboard. Reaching inside, she pulled out a small wicker box and carried it across to her armchair. "Now," she said, "hand me that jacket and I'll see what I can do."

Seb watched Mrs Thompson slip on her reading glasses and reach into her little box for a spool of black thread. She pulled a needle from a little pincushion and threaded a length of black thread onto it. As she worked, the rhythmic ticking of the large clock soothed Seb's nerves.

"Mrs Thompson?"

"Yes, Seb?" She lifted her head and smiled.

"Are you a Christian... I mean, are you saved?" he asked.

Mrs Thompson's hand stilled, then she reached up and pulled off her glasses. "Why, Seb!" she exclaimed. "I am! I was saved when I was about your age through the words of John chapter three and verse sixteen." She paused. "And what about you, Seb?" she asked.

"Yes, I'm saved..." Suddenly what had happened earlier came crashing into his thoughts. He frowned. "Actually, I'm not really sure anymore."

"And why aren't you sure?" Mrs Thompson leaned forward, a concerned look on her wrinkled face.

Seb took a deep breath. "Today I did something that I shouldn't have done. At least, someone who is a Christian wouldn't do it."

Mrs Thompson nodded slowly. "Tell me, Seb, how did you get saved?"

"Well, that's another long story, but I ended up in a dangerous situation and it made me realise that I was a sinner. My friend quoted the verse 'the blood of Jesus Christ His Son cleanses us from all sin' and I realised that, even though I had committed so many sins, the Lord Jesus Christ died for me."

"And you trusted Him."

"Yes."

"First John chapter one and verse seven," said Mrs Thompson, resuming mending. "That's one of my favourite verses. Just think – all sin! There isn't one of my sins that Christ didn't die to put away. Seb, do you see my Bible on the table?"

Seb nodded.

"Go and lift it and turn to that chapter."

Seb followed Mrs Thompson's instructions.

"Now, read from verse eight."

Seb glanced at the Bible and back at Mrs Thompson. "Out loud?"

"Yes, please."

Seb cleared his throat. " 'If we say that we have no sin, we deceive ourselves, and the truth is not in us. If we confess our sins, He is faithful and just to forgive us our sins and to cleanse us from all unrighteousness. If we say that we have not sinned, we make Him a liar, and His word is not in us.' " Seb looked up. Did this mean…?

"So, Seb," said Mrs Thompson, "what do you think of that?"

Seb bit his lip. It was written in black and white – Christians sin. If they say they don't sin, they are lying. But it couldn't include losing one's temper and hitting someone, could it?

"Whatever it is that you've done, you need to confess it to God. But the Bible says that He is faithful and just to forgive us and cleanse us. Read the first verse of the next chapter."

Seb looked down at the Bible again. " 'My little children, these things I write to you, so that you may not sin. And if anyone sins, we have an Advocate with the Father, Jesus Christ the righteous.' "

"Do you know what an Advocate is?"

Seb shook his head. "Not really."

"An Advocate is an intercessor, someone who pleads on behalf of someone else. And that's the Lord Jesus Christ Himself!"

"He's pleading for me?" Seb asked, eyes wide.

"Yes," replied Mrs Thompson. "And it goes on to explain that He was also the sacrifice to atone for our sins, so we are certain that God will not punish us. And," she smiled, "remember your verse – His blood cleanses from *all* sin! Do you think that Christ died for only some of your sins?"

Seb shook his head. Of course not!

Mrs Thompson bent over her sewing again and Seb bowed his head and silently confessed his sin to God. He thanked Him for Christ's death, how His blood cleanses from all sin, and for the Advocate. He laughed with the joy of restored communion with His heavenly Father.

"Seb, a few more verses, then I want to teach you a little hymn. The gospel of John this time, chapter ten and verses twenty-seven to thirty."

Seb rustled through the well-worn pages until he came to the passage. He didn't have to look hard for the verses – they were all underlined in red.

" 'My sheep hear My voice, and I know them, and they follow Me. And I give them eternal life, and they shall never perish; neither shall anyone snatch them out of My hand. My Father, who has given them to Me, is greater than all; and no one is able to snatch them out of My Father's hand. I and My Father are one.' "

"There you go, Seb," said Mrs Thompson, smiling. "Once you are saved, you are always saved. You can never lose your salvation. Never forget that!"

Seb shook his head in wonder. "Thank you so much, Mrs Thompson!"

"You're welcome," she replied. "Now, do you know the hymn 'Before the throne of God above'?"

Seb bit his lip. He didn't think so. It didn't sound familiar.

Mrs Thompson pulled a little pair of scissors from her box and snipped the ends of the thread. She stood up and handed the jacket to Seb. "There you go," she said. "It's the best I can do. The mended sleeve might be a wee bit tighter than the other one."

Seb looked at the jacket. He could hardly see where it was stitched at all. It was certainly a much better job than his mother would have done!

Mrs Thompson was rummaging in a drawer. She pulled out a black hymnbook and flicked through the pages. "Here we are," she said, handing it to Seb. "I love all of this hymn, but especially verse three."

She began to softly sing.

> *"Because the sinless Saviour died,*
> *My sinful soul is counted free,*
> *For God the just is satisfied*
> *To look on Him and pardon me."*

Verse two had caught Seb's attention.

> *When Satan tempts me to despair,*
> *Telling of evil yet within,*
> *Upward I look, and see Him there,*
> *Who made an end of all my sin.*

That's exactly what had happened today. Satan had tempted him to despair, and he had succumbed to the temptation. But God had turned the day around. He still needed to properly apologise to Tyler – he hadn't been in English class and Seb assumed he'd gone home. Tyler might not forgive him. Seb could still be in danger, but now that he knew that God forgave him, he had a peace that nothing could destroy.

Chapter Five

Seb flopped backwards onto his bed, hands behind his head, and kicked off his shoes. The window was open and he could hear the Sunday evening traffic on the main road. A door opened nearby and the strains of the hymn they'd sang that evening floated in the window.

> "The Lamb of God for sinners died,
>
> A victim on the tree;
>
> He gave Himself a sacrifice,
>
> To set the guilty free..."

He smiled. Mrs Thompson, out watering her plants. God had been looking after him; not only did he have a Christian lady right next door; he also had a gathering of believers at the end of his street!

"I never saw a church at the end of the street, Mrs Thompson," he'd said, when she'd told him.

"Ah, but, Seb, it's at the *other* end of the street, not the end where we go to get the bus," she replied.

And when Seb went with Mrs Thompson earlier today, there it was. Situated on the corner, behind a low wall topped with black wrought-iron railings, with a large blue sign proclaiming 'CHRIST JESUS CAME INTO THE WORLD TO SAVE SINNERS.'

Seb adjusted the pillow beneath his head and smiled. Even though it was his first time there, and even though the majority of the people were around Mrs Thompson's age, he'd felt right at home. They weren't all old, however. There was also a young family with three small boys, and a student doctor on placement. They had all welcomed him with open arms. He was looking forward to telling Uncle Matt and Aunt Karen about how God had provided for him.

He jumped, banging his elbow against the wall. He must have drifted off to sleep. And what was that noise? He blinked and rubbed his eyes. His phone! He leaned over the edge of the bed and ran his hand over the carpet. It was half hidden underneath his bed. Lifting it, he noticed the name of the caller.

"Hi, Uncle Matt!"

A deep chuckle came through the phone. "Hi, Seb! I thought you weren't going to answer the phone. Am I phoning at a bad time?"

"Oh, no! It's a really good time, actually. I just got back from the gospel service about half an hour ago, and I'm lying on my bed. I didn't realise I'd fallen asleep until you phoned."

Uncle Matt laughed heartily. "I'm not sure anyone realises they've fallen asleep until they wake up, Seb!"

Seb laughed. "You're right. That's like something Vinnie would come out with!"

"So how are you?" asked Uncle Matt. "You mentioned being at a service – did you find a church nearby?"

"Right at the end of my street, Uncle Matt! Mrs Thompson next door is a believer, and she goes there."

"That's amazing, Seb. God has surely provided for you. It's an answer to prayer."

Seb agreed.

"So how has school been going?" asked Uncle Matt.

Seb paused. He hadn't really thought much about school today. "Well… " he began. "It's been challenging."

"In what way, Seb?" Uncle Matt sounded concerned.

Seb filled him in on the details – about telling his friends he was a believer, Mr Symons' reaction to the news, and the happenings at Friday lunchtime. He mentioned Tyler's brother's threats, and Mrs Thompson's wise counsel. "But I haven't told Mum," he finished by saying. "She's been working all weekend and I've barely seen her. I think she has plenty to worry about anyway, without all of that."

"I know you think that, but she'll find out sooner or later, and it's better if she hears it from you. She'll see the jacket sleeve, after all."

"I guess you're right, Uncle Matt," Seb replied. "I suppose I'm reluctant to tell her because she's said a few times that I have changed, and if I admit I still have problems with my temper, she'll think that salvation doesn't work."

Uncle Matt gave a little chuckle. "Actually, Seb, I think the fact that you have remorse about it will show that salvation does work. It's one of the characteristics of a believer, that when they sin they are miserable, whereas an unsaved person can sin comfortably."

Seb pondered that. "That makes sense, Uncle Matt!" he suddenly exclaimed. "I never thought of that before."

"Now," said Uncle Matt, changing the subject, "everyone here misses you badly and the general consensus is that you have to come some weekend very soon for a visit."

Seb could hear a voice shouting in the background.

"Lavinia says to tell you that the cows have started to calve and that Mirabelle is due in the next few weeks. What's that, Vinnie? Oh, she says you aren't a real farmer until you've helped calve a cow!"

Seb chuckled. He'd love to be back at Cherryhill, helping with the farm work, eating Aunt Karen's delicious meals and enjoying the banter with his cousin, Lavinia, and his friends, Caleb and Rebekah. "I'd love to come some weekend, Uncle Matt," he said.

"Okay, I'll get Karen to phone your mum someday and arrange it. And... what is it, Martha?"

A whispery little voice came through the phone. "Hello, Seb."

Seb smiled. It was his four-year-old cousin. "Hi, Martha! How are you?"

"I'm okay. Daddy didn't tell you about Glen."

Glen. The collie pup that he had chosen and named. The little runt.

"He's got reeeaaally big! He eats loads! Daddy says he's a good dog, but he still swings on Jess's tail."

Seb laughed. "Poor old Jess," he said. "Are all the rest of the pups away?"

"Yep!" replied Martha. "Moss went to Harveys' and Tommy and Madge got one too. They called it Sweep. It chews *everything*."

Seb laughed. He couldn't imagine Madge running around after a mischievous pup.

"I have to go to bed now. Night night, Seb."

"Night night, Martha," Seb replied. He heard a rustle and low voices.

Uncle Matt's voice came through the phone again. "Martha has really taken to Glen. He really has grown a lot; you'd never think he'd been the runt. I think he'll be a good worker too. Good choice, Seb!"

Seb smiled. He had chosen Glen because he had reminded him of himself – small, unwanted and forgotten. But now things were looking up for them both.

He said his goodbyes and dropped the phone back onto the floor. He couldn't wait to get back to Cherryhill. Belfast was another world, but, for the time being, this was Seb's world. This was where God wanted him to be, and, for now, that was enough.

Seb heard the key turn in the lock and the door open. Mum was home from her long day at work as a hospital care assistant. He heard her rummage around, then heard water running in the kitchen and the kettle begin to boil. Footsteps sounded on the stairs and she went into her bedroom. A few minutes later, she rapped lightly on Seb's door.

"Come in," he called.

The door opened slightly and Mum poked her head into the room. She smiled when she saw Seb lying sprawled on the bed, Bible beside him. "How did you get on today?" she asked.

"I'd a good day," he replied. "Mrs Thompson made me dinner. It was almost as good as Aunt Karen's Sunday dinner."

Mum chuckled. "You're always thinking about your stomach, Seb! I'm glad you had a good day anyway. I'm just going to get a cup of tea and some toast. Want some?"

Seb pushed himself off the bed. "I'd love some toast and…is there any of Mrs Thompson's jam left?"

"Not a lot. You've been hard on that jam!"

Seb grinned and followed Mum down the stairs. "Hey, Mum!"

"Yes?"

"Uncle Matt phoned. They want me to go and visit some weekend. Aunt Karen's going to phone you someday."

"That's fine, Seb. I'm sure you'd like to go back for a visit." She slid two slices of bread into the toaster and pressed the lever.

"It feels like ages since I was there," Seb commented, pulling mugs and plates from the cupboard.

Mum nodded. "It seems far removed from the hustle and bustle of city life, doesn't it?"

"Do you like living in the city?" Seb asked.

Mum shrugged. "It's been so long since I lived in the country that it would seem strange to move back. I like the way we can walk to the shops, and there are frequent buses. But I guess it would be nice to have the peace and quiet and have a bit more space."

"Do you think...?"

"Do I think what, Seb?" The toast bounced up and Mum put a slice on each plate.

"Could we ever move to the country?" Seb lifted knives, butter and jam and followed Mum to the table in the living room.

"I thought you might ask that sometime," she admitted, setting down the toast and going back for the tea. "The thing is," she continued, pulling out a chair and sitting down, "while houses can be cheaper to rent in the country, the buses are so infrequent that it'd be difficult getting to work and I really can't afford to buy a car. That's even if I could drive."

Seb looked at her, puzzled. "Did you never learn? I thought most people in the country learned to drive."

Mum shook her head sadly. "I had a couple of lessons before I left home, but I never had any more after that."

"What age were you when you left home?" asked Seb.

"I was seventeen." Mum sighed, then took a sip of her tea. "Old enough to know better, but certainly too young to be away on my own."

"Why did you leave anyway?" Seb asked. It was something he'd been puzzling over for the past number of weeks. By all accounts, Mum's parents had been good people. Aunt Karen had never felt the need to leave home.

Mum bit her lip. "The underlying reason was that I felt hemmed in at home. Mum and Dad were good parents, they sheltered us from many things, but I resented that and wanted to see what was out there. I'd been at the local college and there was a girl I was friendly with whose dad lived in Belfast. She decided to move there to live, and I went with her. I didn't tell my parents or Karen that I was leaving. They all came back from church one night and I was gone."

Seb looked at his mum in amazement. How could she leave a caring home and loving parents like that and never even say goodbye?

"Did you ever see them again?"

"I saw Karen a few times, but that day I took you to Cherryhill, that was the first I'd seen her for quite a number of years. My parents..." A shadow passed across her face. "Yes, I did, once, but it wasn't a joyous reunion, to say the least." She looked down and toyed with the handle of her mug.

It was obvious to Seb that Mum didn't want to talk about her past anymore.

"Anyway," she said, lifting her head and straightening her shoulders, "I can't drive and I can't afford a car or lessons, so we're stuck here for now." She smiled bravely. "I hope school is going okay for you this year," she added.

Seb nodded. "I've a lot to catch up on, but I'll work hard."

"I know you will. It's like I've got a different son now."

Seb bit his lip, remembering Uncle Matt's advice. "Mum?"

"Yes, Seb? What is it?" Mum noticed his hesitancy and looked concerned.

"There's something I likely should tell you, but I don't want you to be alarmed or worried, and I'm really sorry about this, but Uncle Matt said I should be honest with you…"

"Seb! Now I'm getting really worried! What is it?"

As Seb told the story, Mum's eyes widened, and she paused, mug halfway to her mouth. Finally, she set it down and rubbed her temples. "Oh, Seb!" she exclaimed, when he had finished. "Please be careful, won't you? I mean, in a sense I'm proud of you for standing up for the new boy, but you know the type of people Tyler and his brother are, and you don't want to get on the wrong side of them."

"I know," admitted Seb. He knew all right what type of people Tyler's family were. He knew what Tyler was like himself and he certainly wasn't looking forward to apologising tomorrow.

Seb glanced at the clock on the mantelpiece and yawned. "I'd better get to bed," he said, as he stood up. After making his way upstairs, he changed, cleaned his teeth, then pulled back the covers and got into bed. He could hear the faint murmur of the TV downstairs and a car speeding down the street. He closed his eyes, but his brain was still alert and active. Mum's story kept playing through his mind. Why had she never gone back? Had they ever come looking for her? And why hadn't she seen Aunt Karen for years? Weren't their parents dead? When did they die? What happened? And when did she meet Dad? There were so many unanswered questions. The TV was turned off and the stairs creaked as Mum came to bed. Seb finally dropped into a fitful sleep.

Chapter Six

Seb squeezed through the crowd hanging around the lockers and made his way to the form classroom for registration. He hadn't seen Tyler or Corey yet, but they were often late for school. Seb walked into the classroom, pulled out his usual chair and sat down, dropping his schoolbag on the floor beside him.

Zoe and Madison were sitting in front of him, heads close together, whispering. Zoe glanced around, noticed Seb, and nudged her friend. Madison's eyes went wide and she clapped her hand over her mouth, before proceeding to giggle loudly.

Seb rolled his eyes. Both girls were much too melodramatic and loud, in his opinion. He watched as the two girls proceeded to have some sort of argument. Each seemed to want the other to do something. Finally, they both turned around to look at Seb.

"What do you want to know?" he asked.

They looked at each other and giggled again. "What makes you think we want to know anything?" Madison said.

"I'm not stupid," he replied. "What is it?"

Madison pulled a strand of blonde hair over her shoulder and twisted it around her finger. "We were just wondering if you and

Tyler are still speaking."

So that's what this was all about. "Don't know," he said. "I haven't seen him since Friday lunchtime."

The girls looked at each other again. "I saw him on Saturday," said Zoe, "and he was still really mad at you. He said something about Lee teaching you a lesson...?" She looked at him quizzically.

The girls were obviously fishing for information. He didn't particularly want to answer Zoe's question, but he couldn't lie either. He leaned back in his seat and folded his arms. "What are you trying to find out?" he asked.

Zoe leaned forwards, Madison close beside her. "Did Lee do something?" she whispered conspiratorially.

Seb uncrossed his arms and glanced furtively from side to side, before leaning towards the girls. They looked eager to hear whatever Seb was about to say. "Why do you want to know?" he whispered.

Madison frowned. "Seb!" she whined. "Just tell us!"

"Right, class, it's Monday," Mr Symons' voice sounded from the door. "Let's get this registration over with and then you can get to class. Zoe, Madison, turn round and face the front of the room."

The girls gave Seb a look of frustration, before doing what they were told. Seb breathed a sigh of relief. He didn't particularly want to talk about his encounter with Tyler's brother on Friday.

––––––––

Tyler only turned up at school mid-morning, so it was lunchtime before Seb got a chance to speak to him.

"Tyler, can I speak to you?" he asked, as they made their way to the canteen.

Tyler turned round and sneered at him. "What makes you think I want to speak to you?"

"Come on, Tyler, just a minute."

Tyler shrugged. "Well, speak!"

Seb swallowed. What he wanted to say, he'd have preferred that there wasn't an audience. "I want to apologise for hitting you on Friday," he said, squaring his shoulders and trying to look Tyler in the eye.

Tyler looked confused. "You're saying sorry?"

Seb nodded. "Yes, I'm sorry. I was mad at what you were doing to the new boy, but I shouldn't have hit you."

Tyler blinked and looked puzzled, then laughed. "You're right you shouldn't! But," he glanced at Corey beside him and the crowd gathering around them and raised his voice, "I guess my brother sorted you out for that! Wee bit scared of knives, aren't we?"

The crowd began to murmur with excitement. Seb's heart sank. So much for not saying anything about Lee's threats. Tyler and Corey looked at each other and laughed, then walked off in the direction of the canteen.

Seb was starving, but he didn't want to end up in the queue

directly behind Tyler and Corey, so he headed for the lockers to sort out his books for the afternoon classes. As he rummaged in his bag, a conversation in the next aisle caught his attention.

"Can you believe Seb apologised? He's really different this year."

Seb's hand stilled. It sounded like Jade who was in his geography class.

"I know," came the reply. *Zoe.*

"I think he's got all religious. It's so weird!"

"I wonder what Lee did to him."

"I don't know. If he'd stabbed him, he wouldn't be here, would he?"

"Probably not," said Zoe. "Maybe he didn't actually do anything to him after all."

"Hey, speaking of Seb," Jade's voice took on an excited tone. "Have you seen his dad lately?"

"No. Why?"

"He's one of my dad's mates and he told Dad he's bought a massive new TV and he's talking about buying a car."

Seb frowned. His dad? The last he saw him, he was unemployed and spent most of his money on alcohol. There's no way he would have enough for a new TV, never mind a car!

"Seriously?" asked Zoe. "Has he won the lottery or what?"

"I don't know," replied Jade. "Dad thought it was a bit weird, but he never asked any questions. He said it was better not to know."

The voices faded down the corridor and Seb stood up, books forgotten. Surely his dad hadn't turned to burglary, had he? Come to think of it, the evening he'd phoned Seb he had mentioned something about plenty of money. What was going on?

———

Seb lifted his full tray and looked around the canteen. He didn't have to ask to know that he wasn't welcome at his usual table in the corner with Tyler and Corey. A table with only one occupant caught his eye and he made his way to it. As he set down his tray, the new boy looked up with a slight smile.

"Hi," Seb said, pulling out a seat. "I'm Seb."

The boy nodded. "I know who you are," he told him. "My full name is Edward Lim Chee Meng."

Seb blinked. He'd heard the teachers calling him Edward, but he didn't realise his new friend had such a long name.

Edward Lim Chee Meng looked down at his plate and gave a little smile. "You can call me Edward," he said.

Seb breathed a sigh of relief. "Good to meet you, Edward," he said.

He paused to silently thank God for his food, then tucked in. Edward was looking at him a little strangely, but said nothing.

"So where are you from?" asked Seb, when he had wolfed down

half of his dinner.

"Kuala Lumpur, Malaysia," Edward replied. "We've just moved here. My dad works in IT."

Seb frowned. "I'm sorry," he said. "My geography isn't very good. I'm not sure where Malaysia is."

Edward pulled his phone from his pocket, tapped and swiped the screen a few times, then held it out to Seb. "There's a map of the world, and there," he pointed to a peninsula hanging from southeast Asia, "is Peninsular Malaysia. Another part of Malaysia is over there," he pointed to the north of a large island, "in Borneo."

"And where is the city you are from?"

"Kuala Lumpur." Edward zoomed in on Peninsular Malaysia. "It's there, towards the west, just a little more than halfway down."

Seb nodded. He couldn't imagine what it was like to live in another country, especially one so far away. "What's it like in Malaysia?"

Edward shivered. "Much warmer than here! It's tropical, so it never gets cold like it does here. And this is the end of summer!" He laughed.

Seb grinned. "You'll likely get used to it, but you'll need to wrap up warm when winter comes."

The bell rang, signalling the end of lunchtime. The boys stood up. "Seb?"

Seb looked up from putting his dirty plate and cutlery back on the tray.

"I just wanted to say thank you for helping on Friday." Edward looked down sheepishly.

Seb smiled. "No problem, Edward. I didn't exactly go about it in the right way, but I can't stand to see them treat you like that. It's not fair."

Edward pulled a blue diary from his pocket and consulted his timetable. "Are you in geography next?" he asked Seb.

Seb nodded. "Yes, I am. It's this way."

Edward fell into step beside him. "The timetable says we have PE tomorrow. What do we do in PE?"

"Usually football," he replied. "Sometimes we play rugby or basketball, but we always start off the school year with a game of football."

"Outside?"

Seb nodded.

"What do we wear? The shorts and t-shirt?" Edward looked aghast.

Seb chuckled. "Yes, but don't worry, we do so much running around that we don't notice the cold. You've got the long socks too? And the sweatshirt?"

"Yes," replied Edward. "My parents bought everything on the recommended list."

"That will keep you a bit warmer," said Seb. They'd reached the classroom. Seb put his hand on the door handle and paused. Where was his PE kit? He hadn't seen it in his wardrobe or under the stairs. He'd have to search more thoroughly when he got home. He hoped it still fitted.

———

Spending time in detention wasn't a new thing for Seb. Having been a frequent offender in his previous years in school, he was quite used to the way it worked. He'd figured out long ago that if he did the allocated work as quickly as possible, he would be released. It generally didn't matter how well the work was done.

This time, he took a little more time. Even schoolwork in detention should be done to the best of his ability. He didn't plan to be in detention ever again!

Seb decided to take the long way home. He didn't want to chance running into Lee again on the waste ground. As he passed Mrs Thompson's house, the door opened and a white head poked out. "Hello, Seb!"

"Hi, Mrs Thompson!"

"How was school today?" she asked, smoothing down her purple-hen print apron. "Everything go all right?"

Seb nodded. "Pretty much. I apologised to Tyler."

"And how did that go?" Mrs Thompson's head tilted in concern.

"Okay," Seb answered. "He seemed a bit stunned and then he

just wanted to make fun of me, but I'm glad it's behind me."

Mrs Thompson smiled. "I'm sure you are," she said. "Are you coming in for a wee cuppa before you start your homework?"

Seb shook his head. "I'd love to, Mrs Thompson, but I'm late because I had detention today and I've a ton of homework to do."

Mrs Thompson nodded, then held up a forefinger. "Wait there; let me get you something to help you with your work."

In two minutes she was back with a clear plastic food bag stuffed with cookies. "There you go, freshly baked coconut and sultana cookies."

Seb smiled. "Thank you! They look amazing. I should get lots of work done this afternoon!"

Mrs Thompson laughed and waved a hand to swat the compliment away, then went inside and shut her door.

Seb unlocked the front door, then dumped his schoolbag on the floor. Tearing open the bag, he pulled out a cookie. It was good! Sweet and slightly chewy, just the way he liked them. He walked into the kitchen and poured himself a mug of milk, then carried it to the table. As he ate, he opened his homework diary: geography, an English assignment and – he screwed up his nose – some chemistry. He'd better get started.

Half an hour later, he closed his geography books and stood up to stretch. Maybe he should take a look for that PE kit now. He opened the low door to the small cupboard under the stairs. The vacuum cleaner was taking up most of the space on the floor, so he pulled it out and began to hunt through the bags. Christmas decorations, framed photographs, a jumble of belts, scarves and jewellery, another bag which looked like the contents of Mum's bedside cabinet. No PE kit. He began to haul the bags out and tip them out on the floor, becoming increasingly desperate.

When the living room floor was littered with the remnants of life before this house and no PE kit was seen, Seb headed upstairs to begin the same process with his wardrobe. Once his bedroom was in the same condition as the living room, he sat down on his bed, head in his hands. Mr Baird, the PE teacher, was an ex-army sergeant and he expected perfection from his pupils. To turn up without a PE kit wasn't an option. Anybody who purposely came to school without their kit soon wished they hadn't.

Seb groaned. There was only one place it could be. Somewhere he'd hoped never to set foot in again in his life. He could feel his knees tremble already, and he swallowed hard. Delving into the pockets of his schoolbag, he found a key. He shoved it into his trouser pocket and took the stairs two at a time. When he reached the bottom, he ignored the mess in the living room and walked out the door, locking it behind him. Mum wouldn't be home for ages and, while it was quite a walk to Dad's house, actually retrieving the PE kit shouldn't take long if the coast was clear. But if it wasn't... He took a deep breath and begged God to make his trip uneventful. So many things could go badly wrong. What if he still couldn't find the kit? What if someone spotted him? And, worst of all, what if, instead of being out at the pub, Dad was actually at home?

Chapter Seven

As Seb walked briskly through the streets, he pondered where his PE kit would be. He knew that if it had been in his wardrobe or chest of drawers, Mum would have packed it up with the rest of his clothes. Where had he flung it when he came home from school the last day he had had PE? He tried to remember back to June, when his mum and dad were together, when Gran used to come and stay with him until Mum came home from work, when he was a bitter, rebellious teen. He remembered trying out smoking behind the fence at the railway line, Dad yelling at Mum, Gran going into hospital, Seb almost burning the house down, and then being sent to Cherryhill Farm. It seemed so long ago. Almost as if it had been someone else's life.

"Think, Seb, think!" he told himself. Where on earth could it be? Suddenly, a memory washed over him. Of tipping his kit out of his black sports bag and shoving clothes into it instead. Getting packed for leaving to go to Cherryhill, angry and smarting. Dad yelling at him, still angry about the ruined TV, Mum begging him to hurry as the train would be leaving in half an hour. He remembered drawing his foot back and venting his frustration on the football boots, shorts and t-shirt. He'd slammed his bedroom door and made his way down the smoke-damaged hallway and out the door for the final time.

A drop of water landed on Seb's face. He looked up, surprised. Then another, and another. The rain began to get heavier. He needed to hurry or he'd be drenched. He broke into a run and rounded the corner into the familiar street. He could hear the growls and angry barks of the neighbour's pit bull terrier. His heart began to thump and he slowed his speed. No point in drawing attention to himself by running.

Seb could see the house now. The living room curtains were half shut and one looked as if it was falling down. He couldn't see if Dad was inside, and it wasn't possible to look in the window without making himself obvious if anyone did happen to be there. As he came nearer, he kept close to the inside of the pavement. Reaching the door of the house, he gently tried the handle. In the past, Dad never locked the door if he was at home; Mum had always been the one to creep downstairs to lock up after Dad got in after a late night of drinking. The door was locked. Seb hoped this still meant he was out.

Fishing the key from his pocket, he fitted it in the lock. It turned easily. At least Dad hadn't decided to change the locks for some reason. He gingerly opened the door and listened. No blare from the TV. Good. That meant Dad wasn't at home. He stepped inside and shook the rain from his hair. The smell of stale smoke and alcohol assaulted his nostrils. He grimaced. How had he ever lived with these smells? He'd grown to appreciate fresh air lately.

The door to the living room stood open and Seb glanced into the room. He let out a short laugh. 'Mess' didn't even begin to describe the condition of it. The room had been repainted and redecorated since he last saw it, likely Mum's doing, thanks to the insurance money, but the new coffee table was piled high with newspapers, cigarette boxes, an opened can of beer sat on one corner and the TV remote crowned the pile. A mountain of empty cans lay beside the sofa. But the thing which stood out beyond all else in the room was the TV – it seemed to take up an entire wall. He wondered how Dad could even see the whole screen at once from his favourite position on the sofa without having to stand up and move away. Large speakers sat in two corners of the room. Seb shook his head, a wry smile on his face. The sound would be deafening.

He turned from the living room and headed upstairs. There was no point in taking a tour of the house and risking Dad finding him here; he'd simply run upstairs and retrieve the PE kit, which he assumed would be hiding under the bed.

Seb's bedroom wasn't quite how he had left it in June. Mum had obviously taken as many of Seb's personal belongings as she felt necessary, so there was less clutter than he remembered. The bed, however, wasn't properly made. Instead, the maroon-coloured quilt had been hastily pulled up over the pillow, which was lying at an angle. Mum mustn't have taken the time to worry about mundane things like making the bed when she was moving out.

Seb knelt down to look under the bed. He sneezed. The dust lay thick on the fawn carpet. He could see a few coins, an elastic band, last year's school diary, and right at the corner, where the top of the bed met the wall and the chest of drawers, a blue and yellow football boot. He stuck his head and shoulders underneath the bed and wriggled as far as he could, stretching his fingers until they touched the boot. He worked it closer until he had it in his hand. Where was the other one? It wasn't under the bed, anyway. He slid out from under the bed and crawled around to the other side, before peering under the chest of drawers. A crumpled piece of fabric caught his eye and he reached in and pulled out his PE t-shirt. A quick scan under the wardrobe revealed nothing lurking there, apart from more dust. There was nothing else in the room to look under. He sat back on his heels, wondering where the other boot and his shorts could be. Maybe Mum picked them up and put them in the wardrobe or in one of the drawers.

He stood up and opened the wardrobe. His clothes were all gone, only some old video games were left on the floor, ones he got too old for years ago. The chest of drawers only contained some odds and ends, bits and pieces that made sense to keep at the time, but which quickly lost their value and purpose.

Seb scratched his head. Where could the other boot be? A pair of shorts was easily lost, but a football boot? One football boot wasn't of use to anyone.

Maybe it had got into the airing cupboard by mistake. He opened the door... and froze. He could hear a key in the lock of the front door. Seb's heart sank. Thinking he would only be in and out, he hadn't locked the door behind him. Dad would surely realise something was amiss. Seb stepped back into his room, heart racing, and softly closed the door.

The key was pulled back out and the door opened. "Hello?" Dad's gruff voice sounded through the house. "Anybody here? Amanda?"

Amanda? Who was Amanda? Seb noiselessly dropped to the floor and prepared to slide under the bed. If Dad came searching, he didn't want to be caught.

"Oh, well," he heard Dad mutter. "Must have forgotten to lock it again." Seb heard the rustle of Dad removing his coat and walking into the living room. Soon the blare of a football match filled the house. Seb waited. He would give Dad a few minutes to get settled, then he'd creep downstairs and out. He certainly wouldn't hear anything with that racket going on. Maybe he could even poke his head into the airing cupboard on the way past.

Dad seemed unable to settle that evening. Seb couldn't remember a night when Dad was at home that he didn't plop himself in front of the TV, can of beer in hand, and not move for hours. Whatever was the matter with him? He could hear him trudge from the living room to the kitchen, rummage around there, clear his throat and head back to the living room, before repeating the same process. Each time the living room door opened, Seb froze, waiting for the dull tread of Dad's footsteps on the stairs.

Seb was beginning to think he should just make a move the next time Dad went back to the living room and forget about looking in the airing cupboard, when he suddenly heard a creak. Dad was coming upstairs!

Seb wriggled underneath the bed. He grabbed the edge of the quilt and pulled it partially down over the edge of the bed to hide him. He hoped that Dad's observational skills were no better than they had ever been. Seb had barely pulled his hand back under the bed when the door opened. For the longest time Seb could only see the worn toes of Dad's boots, then the feet moved into the room. Seb held his breath. The dust made him want to sneeze.

"I wonder did the brat come back for something? Pity I missed him," Dad muttered to himself, then turned to leave the room. Seb began to breathe a sigh of relief, but it was halted when he saw the boots turn and march straight to the bed. One boot was drawn back. Seb knew what was coming. Quick as a flash, he anchored himself with his toes and fingers and thrust his body to the right, away from the kick at the quilt. The scuffed toe missed his ribs by inches.

"Huh! You just never know; the brat could have been cowering under there like a frightened mouse," Dad said, a throaty laugh following his words as he made his way back downstairs.

Seb's heart was pounding. Dad didn't know how close to the truth his words actually were. He decided to get out as soon as possible. Maybe now that Dad had searched for an intruder, he would stay in the living room for the rest of the evening.

Seb pressed his hands on the floor and prepared to shuffle out of his hiding place when suddenly the commentating and cheering from the TV stopped. Dad's voice boomed through the sudden silence.

"Hello! Yes, I'm listening."

Seb paused. Dad must be on the phone. He'd have to wait until it wasn't so quiet.

"Sure, I can do that. Where did you say?...A grey Zafira, okay... Blue baseball cap..." A longer pause. "Well, I was expecting more. It's a risky thing to do, and I don't have a car yet... okay, that's more like it... No bother. Bye!"

Seb frowned. What was his dad up to now? There wasn't time to think. The football match resumed and Seb decided to make a run for it. Sliding out from under the bed, he held the football boot and t-shirt tightly against his chest. Opening the door, he glanced out into the hallway and listened. Nothing out of the ordinary. He made his way down the stairs as quickly as he could. Two steps creaked and he winced but kept going, hoping the noise from the speakers would muffle the sound. At the bottom, he paused. The door to the living room stood ajar. If he could just get past without Dad looking around…

A goal was scored and the crowd at the match went wild. Seb reached for the door handle at the same time as he stepped off the bottom step. Pressing down on it, he tried to open the door. It was locked! Of all the times for Dad to begin locking doors. A quick glance down confirmed that he'd also taken the key out. Seb fumbled in his pocket and pulled out his own key, conscious that if Dad turned around, he was standing directly in his line of sight.

He thrust the key into the lock and turned. As he pulled the key out, a movement caught his eye. Dad had leaned forward to lift a tin of beer from the coffee table. Seb opened the door and slipped through. He began to pull the door closed and took a final glance into the living room… and recoiled in shock as his eyes met Dad's. Seb slammed the door and turned and ran, as fast as he could, through the pouring rain. He could hear Dad yelling. "Hey, you! Brat! I *knew* you were here. Spying on me! Just you wait… you and that no good…" The words faded, drowned out by the pounding of Seb's feet on the wet pavement and the erratic *thump-thump* of Seb's heart.

Seb didn't slow down until he reached the corner of his street. He was soaked through and his legs were like jelly. As he walked up the street, he could see a light in his living room window. He groaned.

Mum was home.

"Seb! Where were you?" Mum looked up as he walked into the living room. She was sitting in the middle of the living room floor, the contents of the bags Seb had hurriedly emptied strewn around her. She stood up. "And why are you so wet? What are you holding?"

Seb looked down at his hand. He had forgotten, in his mad dash, that he was carrying anything. "It's part of my PE kit."

Mum shook her head, her face revealing her puzzlement. "Seb, please tell me. What are you doing out in the pouring rain, carrying your PE kit? And what is all this about?" She waved her hand over the mess like a fairy godmother trying to turn a pumpkin and mice into a carriage and horses.

"Sorry, Mum," apologised Seb. "I was looking for something. I thought I'd get it all cleared away before you came home, but I was away for longer than I thought."

Mum shook her head. "Look, why don't you go and get a warm shower. I'll start to tidy this up and you can tell me what happened over a piece of Mrs Thompson's steak and gravy pie."

Seb's eyes lit up. "She sent pie?"

Mum gave a little smile. "Yes, Seb. She did. Now, run upstairs and stop thinking about your stomach for once!"

———

When Seb came down, warm and dry and dressed in clean clothes,

Mum had the mess cleared up. The table was set for dinner and at each place there was a plate with a big slice of pie and some salad.

"Feel better now?" she asked, as she poured Seb a glass of apple and blackcurrant juice.

Seb nodded and sat down at the table.

"So, care to tell me yet what you were doing?" she said, when the last of the pie crumbs and gravy were cleared from the plates.

Seb sighed. "I have PE tomorrow."

"Yes?" Mum looked confused.

"I was looking for my PE kit."

Mum's eyes widened. "Oh, no! Seb, *please* don't tell me you went back to Dad's to get it…" she pleaded.

Seb gave a small nod.

Mum closed her eyes and rubbed her forehead. "Was he at home?"

"Not when I arrived, but he came home. He didn't see me until I was leaving."

Mum had gone pale. "Did he follow you?"

Seb grinned wryly. "Mum, have you forgotten how unfit he is? I ran, but he didn't even try to catch me!"

Mum shook her head and reached across the table. Taking Seb's arm, she gave it a gentle shake. "Seb, promise me you will never go there again. *Promise me!*"

"I don't think I need to go there again. You brought everything else. But, Mum…"

"What is it?"

"I only found my t-shirt and one boot. Mr Baird is going to go crazy."

Mum gave her head a quick shake. "I'll write him a note and we'll get you new stuff on Saturday. I'd be very doubtful that last year's kit would even fit you now anyway. I can't believe I forgot all about PE. I'm so stupid!"

"Don't say that, Mum," said Seb. "I forgot as well." He stood up and took his glass and plate to the kitchen. "I'm going upstairs. I've still some homework to do, then I think I'll have an early night."

"Okay, Seb. I'm glad you're safe. I'll leave your note on the table for tomorrow morning. Sleep well."

"You too, Mum."

Seb climbed the stairs and went into his room. He lifted a refill pad and opened his chemistry textbook to the chapter they had covered that day in school. As he tried to read the questions, his mind kept drifting back to his visit to Dad's house. He was very thankful that he had escaped. But what was that conversation he had overheard? And why did Dad seem to think he was spying on him? What *was* Dad up to?

Chapter Eight

Mr Baird read the note and peered at Seb from under bushy red eyebrows. Seb took a breath and concentrated on standing straight.

"You've *lost* your PE kit." It was a statement of fact, mixed with incredulity.

"Yes, *sir*." Seb pressed his hands to his sides. His right hand felt a compulsive urge to salute.

Mr Baird shook his head. "This is the last time this happens, Mitchelson."

Seb nodded. "Yes, sir." His right wrist twitched and he clenched his fist.

"To the library." He bent down and pulled out a sheet of paper from the filing cabinet beside the desk in the tiny office. "I expect you to report back to me at 1125 hours. You must have this worksheet completed. Understood?"

"Yes, sir!" exclaimed Seb. His right hand rose sharply and the backs of his fingers touched his forehead. Seb groaned inwardly and quickly reached for the page. The last thing he wanted was Mr Baird to think he was making fun of him. He spun around and fled the office, glancing back as he turned the corner. But, rather than look angry, Mr Baird's red moustache seemed to be twitching. Seb knew he'd got off very lightly, but surely Mr Baird wasn't laughing…?

———

Mrs Jones stood on tiptoe and stretched to her full height. Still her fingertips were nowhere near the top of the door. She turned round, a look of determination on her little, round face. Grabbing her chair, she hauled it to the door of the storeroom and kicked off her sensible navy shoes, then proceeded to clamber onto the chair. The extra inches made all the difference and she was easily able to retrieve the pen from the top of the doorframe.

Seb could hear Tyler's audible groan coming from the back of the room. He'd obviously expected Mrs Jones to spend most of the lesson trying to find her pen, rather than teaching them Pythagoras' theorem. He hoped Tyler wouldn't figure out how Mrs Jones had located the missing pen.

The eccentric maths teacher wobbled off the chair, then attempted to shove her feet into her shoes. In the process, she managed to kick one across the room, prompting a roar of laughter from the class. She hobbled over to pick it up and carry it back to her seat.

Both shoes safely on her feet, pen in hand and absentminded smile back on her face, she began to go through the homework questions one by one. And, one by one, Seb put an X beside his answers. He scowled at the page. He simply couldn't understand how algebraic formulae worked. Mrs Jones' explanation made things no clearer. He glanced at Edward, who was sitting at the next desk. His page was full of neat ticks.

The bell rang and the class jumped up and headed for the door. "And do the next twelve questions for the next class, children." Mrs Jones' high-pitched voice was drowned out in the clatter and chatter of hungry teenagers at lunchtime.

Seb shoved his books into his bag and stood up. Edward had opened his diary and was neatly writing down the allocated homework. "Are you coming to the canteen for lunch?" asked Seb.

Edward looked up and smiled. "Yes, in one moment." He finished writing and placed the diary in his blazer pocket, gathered his pens and books and tidied everything away into his schoolbag. Finally, he stood up.

As they left the classroom and made their way down the corridor, Seb turned to Edward. "Can you understand the stuff in maths?"

Edward nodded. "Yes, I can. Mrs Jones' accent is a little hard for me to understand, but I think she explains it clearly."

Seb shook his head. "Really? I can't understand it at all. I got every single one of those questions wrong!"

Edward frowned. "That's not good!"

Seb gave a dry laugh. "It certainly isn't, Edward. But I think it's likely to do with the fact that this is the first year I've actually tried to understand anything."

"Did you not care about school last year?"

"Not care? I hated school. Not just last year, but every year! I think I'm struggling because I don't understand the basic things that I should know."

Edward bit his lip. "Maybe you should talk to Mrs Jones."

"Oh, I couldn't do that! I don't think it would do any good."

Edward was silent. They'd reached the canteen and joined the queue for food. "Well…" he began. He glanced around him and back to Seb. "I could help you, but maybe you'd rather it was someone else."

Seb turned to Edward. "But why? You know way more than anyone else in the class. Why would I rather it was someone else?"

Edward looked down at his feet. "People here don't seem to like me very much."

Seb slowly shook his head. "Edward, I'm sorry that people here are so racist. It's wrong to be nasty to someone because they are different in some way. In God's eyes, none of us are better than anyone else."

Edward raised his eyes to look at Seb and frowned. "But Seb, I'm a Buddhist. I don't believe in your God."

A Buddhist? Seb had barely heard of Buddhism and he'd certainly never met a Buddhist! What could he possibly say to convince his new friend that God was the only true God?

The line moved forward and Edward gestured for Seb to go ahead and order his food.

After they were seated and Seb had silently thanked God for his food, Edward spoke. "Seb, why do you close your eyes before you eat? I thought it might be a tradition of this country, but no one else here does it."

"I'm thanking God for my food," Seb replied simply.

Edward frowned. "Shouldn't you thank the ladies in the kitchen? Or your parents for the money to pay for the food?"

"I guess so. But we receive everything from God: the air we breathe, the food we eat, the clothes we wear, our houses, our health... everything, really."

"Will your God be angry if you don't thank Him?"

Seb smiled, his fork filled with chilli con carne and rice. "God is a God of love. He loves us. The Bible says, 'God so loved the world that He gave His only begotten Son, that whoever believes in Him should not perish but have everlasting life.' "

Edward looked puzzled. "The Bible is your holy book, right?"

"It's God's Word." Seb was about to explain what he meant, but Edward looked ready to burst with more questions.

"It sounds beautiful, but I don't understand. Your God has a son?"

Seb nodded. "Yes, His Son is called the Lord Jesus Christ, but He is also God."

"You have two Gods?"

Seb shook his head. "No. There is the Father, the Son, and the Holy Spirit – but they are One. So we have one God, not three."

"I'm sorry, Seb. I don't understand."

Seb smiled. "Don't worry, Edward, I can't get my head around it either! God is bigger than us; He knows everything, so there are things that are perfectly clear to Him, but we can't quite understand them. But just because we can't understand everything about God doesn't mean that He isn't real. To be honest, I'm glad that God knows way more than I do!"

Edward poked his chicken pie thoughtfully. "But you are a Christian because your parents are Christians."

Seb laughed. "Oh no, Edward, my parents aren't Christians."

"They aren't?" Edward looked surprised.

"Neither of them are Christians, in the true Bible sense of the word. In fact, my dad is an atheist. A Christian is someone who accepts that they have sinned against God, and who realises that God sent His Son to this earth to die for our sins, and trusts Him. Then they are on their way to heaven."

"You...you think you are going to heaven?" Edward looked shocked.

"Edward, I *know* I am going to heaven," Seb replied. "God has said that whoever believes in His Son will have everlasting life – that includes heaven. I believed in His Son, the Lord Jesus Christ, this summer, so that's why I'm sure I'm going there."

"Heaven!" Edward exclaimed. "Only gods are in heaven!"

Seb shook his head. "But there is only one God, and He wants us to be in heaven with Him. The only way we can be sure that's where we're going is if we believe in His Son."

Edward looked puzzled. "But what if someone doesn't believe?"

Seb looked at Edward sadly. He had to be honest. "If someone doesn't believe, they go to hell."

"I know about hell," replied Edward, more confidently. "That's where dead people go. We burn hell money and offerings for our dead relatives."

"Edward, when someone is in hell, they are there forever. It's a terrible place. The only way to be sure you aren't going there is to trust in the Lord Jesus Christ, who died to take the punishment for our sins."

Edward shrugged. "Seb, you have your religion and I have mine, and it will all work out in the end."

Seb leaned across the table. He felt deeply concerned about Edward. He didn't even know about the one true God, or His Son, Jesus Christ. If he never got saved, he would never be in heaven, no matter how nice a person he was. "Edward, it won't all work out in the end. You need to trust Christ!"

Seb suddenly became aware of someone standing behind him.

He turned around to see Madison, who was frowning at Seb. "You can't say that, Seb! Who do you think you are to say that his religion isn't the right one and yours is? There are loads of religions in the world and for you to say that your way is the only way is being plain conceited!"

"But Madison, it *is* the only way! The Bible says it is. Jesus said, 'I am the way, the truth, and the life. No one comes to the Father except through Me.' He's the only way!"

Madison gave a one-shoulder shrug. "There are other religions which say they are the only way. Who's right? Maybe there is no God after all!" She walked off.

Seb sighed. He knew for sure that God was the only God and Christ was the only way to heaven, but how could he prove that? He'd have to think about it.

The bell rang. Seb and Edward stood up and made their way to the next class. Seb remembered Edward's offer of help. "Edward, would you help me with maths sometime?"

Edward smiled. "No problem. In fact, why don't you come to my house tonight and we can do our homework together. You can stay for dinner, meet my family."

Seb considered the offer. Mum was working late tonight and he'd be on his own. It would be nice to meet Edward's family. He only hoped he'd like the food.

"I'd like that," Seb told him.

"Good." He pulled out his phone. "I'll let Mum know you will be coming. She won't mind. She likes meeting people."

When the bell rang to signal the end of the school day, Seb waited for Edward to gather his books. As they left the school, Seb could hear Tyler shouting, "Hey, Seb! What are you doing walking home with Rice-man?" Corey joined in the laughter.

Seb ignored them. He didn't like their choice of nickname for Edward. To them, he was Chinese, and here, Chinese people owned restaurants serving westernised Asian food. They figured that Edward ate nothing but rice.

The boys called taunts and jeers for a while, but soon Edward and Seb turned left and they headed right.

"Why did your family want to move here?" asked Seb.

"My dad got a job in a company as an IT specialist. He wants us to move here permanently. He thinks there are better opportunities for us in the UK."

"What do you miss most about Malaysia?"

Edward adjusted his bag on his shoulders. "I miss the weather. There are some foods we can't buy here and I miss those. But most of all, I guess I just miss being comfortable in my surroundings. It's so different here."

Seb smiled. It wasn't quite the same as moving right across the world, but he certainly knew the feeling of being out of his comfort zone. He didn't exactly feel right at home when he first went to Cherryhill.

"Your English is very good," he told Edward.

Edward laughed. "Yes. We speak English in Malaysia."

"You do? Not Chinese?"

Edward smiled and shook his head. "My ancestors came from China many years ago, but we speak English at home. I know a little Mandarin, but I don't speak it very well. The official language of Malaysia is Malay. We had to speak Malay at school, but we don't use it generally."

Seb was amazed. Here was someone who actually knew more than one language, who'd had the courage to come with his family to an unfamiliar country. Why did Tyler and the other bullies think that they were better than Edward? Seb didn't know if they had ever been out of Belfast very much, let alone Northern Ireland. Who were they to treat him in such a manner?

Edward stopped at a gate and pushed it open. Seb followed, closing the gate behind him and walking down the neat garden path. They reached the door and Edward pulled a key from his pocket and unlocked the door. He pushed it open. "Ma! I'm home!" he called.

Seb felt a flutter of nerves in his stomach. He took a deep breath. He'd never been in the house of someone from another country before. What if Edward's parents took an instant dislike to him? After all, these people were clever and courageous. He was just plain, ordinary Seb.

Edward stood back and smiled. "Come in!" he said. Seb stepped inside.

Chapter Nine

A petite woman with dark, shoulder-length hair and thick-rimmed glasses appeared from one of the doors in the hallway. She smiled when she saw the boys. "Edward! How was your day?" she asked.

"It was good," Edward replied, dropping his bag and reaching down to untie his shoe laces. He reached out a hand to gesture towards Seb. "This is my friend, Seb."

Edward's mum held out a tiny hand to Seb. He reached out and shook it, careful not to squeeze too tightly. He felt as if his hands were as large as Uncle Matt's!

"Pleased to meet you," she said, smiling. "In Malaysia, young people call older people 'uncle' and 'aunt', so why don't you call me Auntie Annie."

Seb smiled politely. Calling a complete stranger 'Auntie' seemed a bit strange to him, but he didn't want to offend his new friend's family. He could hear the zip and thud of a computer game being played somewhere in the house.

"Joseph!" Annie called. "Switch off your game and come get a snack." She walked back up the hallway and through a door. Edward and Seb followed.

The kitchen was bright and airy, the cupboards in a pale oak with a dark worktop. The walls were painted a pale cream and yellow curtains framed the windows. At one end, patio doors opened out onto a well-groomed garden with a central patio. A wooden table was pushed against one wall, and resting on the table was a bowl of small, round, deep pink fruit.

Annie lifted a jug of juice from the fridge and carried it to the table with a stack of glasses. "Have a seat," she told Seb.

A young boy wearing spectacles crashed into the room, then stopped abruptly when he saw Seb. He regarded him curiously. "Are you Edward's friend?" he asked.

Seb nodded. "Yes, I'm Seb."

"I'm Joseph," he told him. "Joseph Lim Chee Hua." His gaze dropped to Seb's feet and his eyes widened. "You haven't taken your shoes off!" he exclaimed.

"Joseph!" exclaimed Annie. "Be polite!"

Seb glanced at everyone else's feet. Sure enough, Edward and Joseph were in their socks, Annie was wearing a pair of soft slippers. "I'm really sorry," he said, reaching down to untie his laces. He wondered if he had lifted a pair of socks without holes in the toes this morning.

"Seb, please don't worry," reassured Annie. "We always take our shoes off indoors, but we are living in your country now."

Seb pulled the shoes off and stood up to carry them to the front door. "Thank you," he told Edward's mum, "but if this is what you do, then I'm happy to do it too." He left the shoes at the front door beside all the other shapes and sizes of footwear. How had he missed noticing them?

As he walked back into the kitchen, he saw Edward and Joseph lifting the fruit from the bowl and peeling the pink-red skin. "These aren't as good as the ones at home," commented Joseph.

"I didn't think they would be, but I was very pleased to find them," replied Annie. She looked up as Seb slid back into his seat. "Help yourself, Seb. These are lychees."

Seb reached for the small bumpy fruit and began to peel it. The skin peeled off easily to reveal soft white flesh. Seb popped it into his mouth. "This is good," he said, as the juicy flesh flooded his taste buds with sweetness.

Edward nodded. "I love lychees. They're very similar to rambutan, which is my favourite fruit. It's like a hairy version of lychee."

"Well, durian is *my* favourite," said Joseph, licking his lips. "I really miss durian."

Annie laughed. "I think we all miss durian, especially your dad. We certainly won't be able to get that here, though."

Seb frowned. "What's that?"

"Durian. It's another fruit," explained Edward. "But it's something that most westerners don't like. It has a really strong smell which tends to put people off before they even eat it."

"But it's really delicious!" exclaimed Joseph.

"It is," agreed Edward wistfully.

"What does it look like?" asked Seb. How could there be so many varieties of fruit in the world that he had never even heard of?

Edward cupped his hands as if he were holding an imaginary round object. "It's maybe a little bigger than a large pineapple, it's a yellow-green colour and has spikes. When you break it open, it has a few big seeds, and the flesh is soft and pale yellow."

It sounded very strange to Seb.

"It's kind of sweet, but with a taste of onions."

"Onions!" exclaimed Seb.

Edward laughed. "It leaves an aftertaste as well and everyone around can tell you've been eating it because of the smell."

Seb shook his head. "It doesn't sound very appealing!"

Annie chuckled. "It's actually very addictive," she said. "Maybe someday you'll visit Malaysia and you can try it out."

Seb visit Malaysia? He couldn't ever see that happening. Malaysia was so far away!

When all that was left of the lychees was a bowl of deep pink skins and shiny brown stones, Seb and Edward spread their books out on the kitchen table. Joseph returned to his bedroom and the whizzing and zapping sounds resumed.

Edward was very patient and finally Seb began to understand the workings of algebraic formulae.

"Now, let's do the last question and we won't compare answers until we have finished, okay?"

Seb nodded. Could he really do this on his own?

A few minutes later, he looked up from his page. "I have an answer..."

"Let me see." Edward reached out his hand for the page. As he glanced at it, he broke into a large smile. "You did it!" he exclaimed, as he bumped his fist against Seb's.

"I did?" asked Seb, unbelievingly. He smiled. "That's great! Thanks, Edward."

"No problem," he answered.

As they completed a short business studies assignment, Annie began to chop meat for dinner.

"Pa will be home soon," Edward told Seb as they tidied their books into their schoolbags. "He doesn't have to work such long hours in this country."

They left their bags at the front door and went into the lounge. Two cream leather sofas faced each other over a dark wooden coffee table. A TV sat in one corner and in the other...

"What's that?" asked Seb, pointing towards an ornately carved table. An oriental figurine sat cross-legged on the table top behind a china bowl. Plates of fruit and cups containing liquid sat around it, and a gold-edged frame with Chinese characters on a red background sat to one side. At the other side was a tall cylinder with red-tipped sticks protruding from the top.

Edward glanced across the room. "That's an altar," he told Seb.

An *altar*? Seb's eyes widened. To an idol? He could hardly believe his eyes. Of course, he knew that idols and altars existed, but to think that his friend, who had helped him with his maths homework and seemed so...so *normal*, actually had idols in his house. "What's the food about?" he asked.

"Oh, we offer food for those in the spirit world. It will help us have a better re-birth because it helps us release selfishness."

"A re-birth?"

"Yes, when we die we are reincarnated and come back to earth as someone or something else – depending on how we lived here, of course."

Seb stared at Edward. "You believe that?" he asked.

"Of course," he replied. "My parents believe that and so do I."

Seb was astounded. He'd heard of reincarnation, but had never really thought that anyone actually believed it. He couldn't understand how someone as intelligent as Edward could think that they would return to earth after they were dead, only as another person. It didn't make any sense to him.

A key turned in the front door. "It's Pa," said Edward, getting up to greet his father as he came into the room. "Pa, this is my friend, Seb. Seb, this is my father."

Seb shook his hand. Straight, black hair fell over the man's forehead. He was a slightly taller version of his son. "Pleased to meet you, Mr..." he trailed off. He couldn't remember Edward's surname. Or should he be calling him 'Uncle'?

The man smiled. "Lim. Lim Yoon Seng, but you can call me Uncle Lim."

Seb nodded. He hadn't quite caught the man's name, and couldn't understand why he had only a Chinese sounding name, when the rest of the family had names he was familiar with. And, come to think of it, wasn't Lim actually Edward's surname? Why was Edward's surname the same as his father's first name? Seb was thoroughly confused.

A delicious aroma wafted from the kitchen. Annie appeared, holding a wooden utensil and wearing a black apron. "Dinner is almost ready," she said. "Please come through to the kitchen."

Seb's stomach growled. He was hungry and the food smelled good. He followed the others to the kitchen and took the seat he was offered. Joseph came racing into the kitchen and skidded along the floor to his seat. Mr Lim raised an eyebrow at his son. "Sorry, Pa!" he said as he pulled out his chair and sat down.

Annie carried plates of steaming food to the table. She passed them around and sat down. No one began to eat.

This is odd, thought Seb. It was almost as if they were waiting to give thanks for the food!

Joseph cleared his throat. "Pa, eat," he said, then turned to Annie.

"Ma, eat." He glanced between Seb and Edward, and shrugged. "Seb, eat. Edward, eat."

Edward then spoke. "Pa, eat. Ma, eat. Seb, eat."

Seb blinked. What was all that about? The family lifted their spoons and forks and began their meal. Seb reached for his, then remembered that he hadn't thanked God for his food. He bowed his head.

As he lifted his head, he looked up to see all eyes on him. He smiled nervously. Edward's father smiled back. "We have our customs, you have yours." Seb bit his lip. How would he explain to this man that it wasn't just a custom?

Before he could formulate a response, Mr Lim was asking Edward about his day. Seb dug his fork into the food on his plate – some sort of meat in a brown-coloured sauce, and the finest, whitest noodles he'd ever seen in his life.

"Do you like it?" asked Annie as he swallowed.

"It's delicious!" Seb exclaimed. "What is it?"

Annie smiled. "It's called daging masak kicap, beef cooked with a sauce called kicap manis – a sweet Malaysian type of soy sauce."

"What sort of noodles are these?"

"Oh, those are glass noodles," explained Annie, excitedly. "I couldn't believe it when I found them in the supermarket here."

"They sell them here? In Belfast?" asked Seb.

"Yes! And the kicap manis."

"Are there things you can't get?"

Annie sighed. "Apart from rambutan and durian we were talking about earlier, there are lots of fruits and vegetables we can't find. Pastes and different ingredients for the old recipes that my mother and grandmother made..." She looked wistful, then smiled. "But we're glad to be here. This country will have so many more opportunities for Edward and Joseph."

Seb took another mouthful of food. The greatest opportunity for this family would be to hear the good news that Christ died for their sins, that no longer would they need to burn incense and offer food to a lifeless idol, but that by trusting in the Lord Jesus – being truly born again – they would be sure of heaven at the end of life. This was his greatest desire and he prayed that he would have an opportunity to witness to them of God's wonderful, all-encompassing love.

Chapter Ten

"All right, class," intoned Mr Kerry. "You should all have read Act One of Romeo and Juliet for today. We are going to look at two groups of people: the Montagues and the Capulets..."

Seb yawned and looked out the window. A blue-boilersuited man was cutting the grass on a red ride-on lawnmower and Seb could see a rugby match in progress on the sports field. The class murmured and chattered and a bluebottle buzzed lazily around the room. Seb turned his attention back to Mr Kerry and tried to concentrate on what he was saying. Romeo and Juliet held no interest whatsoever for Seb, and he failed to see the point in studying an ancient story where everyone seemed obsessed with murder and death. Even the main characters died at the end! Seb wondered if Mr Shakespeare couldn't figure out what to do with them so he just killed them off.

"...the families were having a feud. Any ideas what this feud was about?" Mr Kerry surveyed the room. He had a peculiar habit of rubbing his right elbow while he was waiting for answers, almost as if he had banged it on something.

No one acknowledged that he had spoken, so Mr Kerry stopped rubbing his elbow and answered his own question. Seb wondered yet again if the person who had been in charge of the timetable had secretly held a grudge against his class. English, taught by Mr Kerry, last thing on a Friday afternoon, was akin to torture.

As Mr Kerry droned on about friction and deep-seated resentment between families, Seb's mind drifted back over the past couple of weeks. He'd been back to Edward's a few times, and once, on Mum's day off, Edward had visited his house. They'd had a few good discussions about religion.

"Why is your religion better than all the others?" Edward had asked one day, as they walked home from school.

"It's not really about it being *better*, or even that it's a religion at all. It's the only way to get to heaven," Seb replied.

"But how are you so sure?" Edward persisted.

Seb had been pondering this question ever since the day that Madison had accused him of being conceited. The answer had dawned on him during the service on Sunday evening, when the speaker had read First Corinthians fifteen and verses three and four – "... Christ died for our sins according to the Scriptures, and... He was buried, and... He rose again... according to the Scriptures..."

"Edward, it's because the Lord Jesus Christ is alive! He died, but He rose from the dead. There are no religions that worship a man who is still alive. Buddha, Confucius, Mohammed... they all died. And they all stayed dead! The Lord Jesus Christ rose from the dead and went to heaven forty days later. People watched Him go."

"But how do you know His resurrection wasn't simply a made-up story? Maybe He didn't really die."

Seb smiled. "Have you ever read the Bible?" he asked.

Edward shook his head. "I don't have a Bible."

"I'll get you one," Seb told him, "then you can read through it. The arguments that people put up – such as that He only fainted, or that He did die but people stole His body – really don't work. I mean, the soldiers, who were used to crucifying people, knew He was dead, because when they were told to break His legs to hasten death, they didn't do it, and instead pierced His side with a spear. And when they did that, blood and water flowed out, proving that He was already dead. And no one could have got near the tomb to steal His body because there were soldiers guarding the tomb."

Edward looked thoughtful. "Yes, I would like to read this book you talk about so much."

So the next day Seb had called at Mrs Thompson's house when he came home from school.

"Seb! Good to see you. Are you coming in for some banana bread?"

Seb could smell the delicious aroma wafting from the kitchen. His stomach rumbled. "I'd love some banana bread, Mrs Thompson!"

He followed Mrs Thompson into the house and sank onto her sofa. She disappeared into the kitchen and returned with a tray containing banana bread and tea.

"Now, Seb," she said, when they had begun to tuck into the soft, sweet bread. "Were you just coming to see me, or did you have something you wanted to ask me?" She frowned. "You haven't been in trouble with those boys again, have you?"

Seb shook his head. "Oh, no, Mrs Thompson. I haven't met Lee since that day you sewed up my jacket. And Tyler and Corey just ignore me now. It's as if I'm not even worth speaking to anymore."

Mrs Thompson nodded. "They likely can see the light in you, and they don't like it. It says in John's Gospel that those who practise evil hate the light and don't come to the light, lest their deeds should be exposed. The light in you exposes their wicked deeds."

Seb shrugged. He wasn't sure if that was the reason, but whatever it was, he wasn't really sorry they were keeping their distance. Seb scraped the last few brown crumbs from the plate and popped them in his mouth. "Mrs Thompson," he said, as he set down his fork, "I have a friend who has just moved here from Malaysia with his family. He's a Buddhist, but I've been telling him about the Lord Jesus Christ. He says he'd like a Bible, but I only have the one that Uncle Matt and Aunt Karen gave me. Do you have a spare Bible, or could you get me one for him?"

Mrs Thompson gave a little laugh and stood up. "Seb, I have a whole box of Bibles! I like to give one to anyone who asks me. It would be a pleasure to give one to your friend." She opened the cupboard under the stairs and rummaged in a cardboard box. Pulling out a black, leather-bound Bible, she handed it to Seb. "What is your friend's name?" she asked.

"Edward Lim," replied Seb. He still hadn't worked out why there were two more names after his surname, but that was what the teachers called him.

"I'll be praying for him," Mrs Thompson assured him. "God makes no mistakes. That family moved here for a reason, and maybe it was to hear the gospel."

––––––

The bell rang and Seb jumped. He had been so busy thinking of Edward and the Bible that he had completely missed the rest of Mr Kerry's lesson. He turned to Zoe, who was frantically stuffing her books into her bag. "Did Mr Kerry give any homework?" he asked. "My mind kind of wandered."

Zoe laughed. "Something about comparing and contrasting the Montagues and the Capulets," she answered. "But I think he said we had a week to do it." She gathered her file and raced after Madison, who was almost at the door. "Have a good weekend," she called over her shoulder.

Seb smiled. He'd been looking forward to this weekend. He glanced at his watch. He had just one hour to get home, pack his bag and make his way to the train station. He couldn't wait to get to Cherryhill again. It seemed like months, rather than a few weeks, since he'd been there.

He slung his bag over his shoulder and joined the crowd who were pushing and shoving for the door. Almost everyone was in a rush; no one wanted to waste a minute of the precious weekend. They poured out of the school gates in every direction. Seb turned left and walked briskly. He pulled out his homework diary as he walked and opened it to next week. This year, he'd tried to do all his homework as soon as he could, so most of the homework due for Monday was already completed. The only exception was a set of maths questions, which Mrs Jones had given today. Hopefully he could do them on the train. He didn't want to spend time at Cherryhill doing maths homework.

The roads were heavy with traffic and initially Seb didn't notice the green Ford Focus which seemed to be crawling along at the same pace as Seb was walking. He couldn't see the driver; the windows appeared to be tinted. It wasn't until he turned into a quieter street that he began to be alarmed. The car turned into the street as well. It drove slowly past Seb, then pulled to a stop outside the entrance to the football grounds. Seb frowned. Surely the car wasn't following him, was it?

Seb slowed his steps. After his encounter with Lee, he didn't want to take any chances. Up ahead, on the opposite side, a narrow street turned off between two houses. Seb crossed the road and darted up the alley. He could hear the whine of the car reversing and he began to run. The alley was just wide enough for a car, but not wide enough for Seb as well. If the car followed him, Seb would be in danger of being run over.

He reached the end of the alley and turned left. He spotted another narrow street and turned right, then left again. He stopped to listen and catch his breath. Nothing. He was quite sure he had lost his pursuer. All the same, he decided to be cautious. Taking a few extra twists and turns, he finally reached his house. As he glanced at his watch, he groaned. He had lost ten valuable minutes.

He turned the key in the door and flung it open. Racing upstairs, he ran into his room and began to pull clothes from the drawers. What did he need?

Ten minutes later, he hoisted the bag and ran back downstairs. As he was locking the door, he remembered his maths homework. He paused. Should he go back for it? Surely it wouldn't matter for once...

He sighed. To deliberately not do his homework was wrong. He opened the door again and bolted up the stairs. He grabbed his maths book, a refill pad and his pencil case.

After locking the door for a second time , he glanced at his watch – thirteen minutes to get to the train station, a twenty-minute walk away. Seb broke into a run.

———

The train pulled into the station. Seb was already out of his seat, ready to press the button to open the doors. He had breathed a sigh of relief that he had made it to the station in time. He had barely stepped onto the crammed Friday evening train before the doors beeped and shut. After a few stops he had managed to find a seat and was able to complete ten out of the twelve maths questions.

The train jerked to a stop and Seb stepped out, then made his way to the exit. He could see Uncle Matt and Martha waiting for him. Matt was leaning against a pillar, brawny arms folded, as if he had all the time in the word. Martha was hopping impatiently from foot to foot. As he approached, Matt pushed off from the pillar and walked towards him.

"Well, Seb," he said, a genuine smile splitting his face. "You made it!"

"I nearly didn't!" Seb told him. He held up a finger and thumb a hair breadth apart. "I was this close to missing the train."

Uncle Matt smiled. "I hope you had a chance to catch your breath – Vinnie is starting the milking and I think she's expecting some help when we get back!"

The journey to Cherryhill was the same route that Uncle Matt had taken the day that Seb first arrived, away back at the beginning of the summer. But this time, instead of marvelling at the remoteness, Seb feasted his eyes on the green fields with cattle and sheep, the isolated and scattered farms and the winding roads. Finally, they turned in the lane to Cherryhill. Seb smiled as the familiar ivy-covered farmhouse came into view. He couldn't help but feel that he'd just come home.

Chapter Eleven

Two dogs ran from the direction of the outbuildings, one a large black and white collie, the other a long-legged pup. Seb laughed. "Look how big Glen is!" he exclaimed. He tumbled out of the jeep and braced himself as the pup threw himself at Seb, then proceeded to chew his laces. Seb picked him up, and Glen set to work licking his face, his black tail wagging at great speed.

Martha watched the reunion, her hands clasped behind her back. "He remembers you, Seb," she told him, blue eyes serious. "I told him about you every day. I didn't want him to forget."

Seb smiled at his little cousin. "Thank you, Martha," he said, setting Glen down. "It definitely worked."

She smiled and crouched down to pat Glen's head. He twisted his head to playfully bite at her hand and she lifted a finger to scold him. "No, Glen, that's not nice. Remember, we're not allowed to bite!"

Aunt Karen greeted Seb with a hug and a blueberry muffin. "I've left your farming clothes on your bed and your wellies are at the back door. But take your time. Matt will go and help Lavinia until you're ready. Or… maybe you'd rather not help with the milking?"

Seb wolfed down the muffin. "Are you kidding?!" he exclaimed.

"I've been dying to get back to the milking parlour!"

Aunt Karen chuckled. "Well, when you get back in we'll have dinner. I think Lavinia has a bit of homework to finish up afterwards."

Seb scrunched his nose. "Me too," he said. "I got most of it done on the train, but I need to get it finished."

He excused himself and ran upstairs to change. Soon he was making his way to the milking parlour across the yard. He slid back the red door and moved past the stainless steel tank. He could hear the loud hum of the milking machine. He slid the inner door aside and closed it behind him.

Lavinia looked up from removing the clusters from one of the cows. A smile broke across her face. "Hey, Seb!" she called above the noise.

Seb made his way down the steps. "Hi, Vinnie," he replied. Uncle Matt sprayed the cows' teats with disinfectant solution. Seb opened the gate to let them out, then grabbed a wad of blue roll and folded it over a few times.

"How are you?" asked Lavinia, as she watched Seb wiping the udders of the next batch of cows.

"Good!" he replied. "It's great to be back. I've missed this." He inhaled deeply. "Cows – it's the best smell on earth!"

Lavinia threw back her head and laughed. "You certainly didn't think that when you first came here. I thought you were going to be sick!"

Seb smiled. He really did like the smell. It reminded him of happy times, of laughter, of good, honest work. Suddenly he remembered. "Is Mirabelle through yet?"

Lavinia's eyes widened. "Wait and see!" She looked as if she wanted to say more, but clamped her lips shut instead.

Seb was puzzled. He thought perhaps Lavinia wanted to see if Mirabelle recognised him. He dropped the wad of paper towels in the bin and began to remove the clusters from the opposite row of cows.

———

After a dinner of steak and chips, followed by strawberry meringue pudding, Seb and Lavinia spread their books out on the kitchen table. Lavinia was working on a history assignment. "My history teacher is so cruel!" she exclaimed melodramatically. "Imagine giving us all this homework on a Friday." She waved a hand over her books, before glancing at Seb's maths. "How much do you have to do?"

"Just two maths questions," he replied.

"Two questions!" she exclaimed indignantly. "Is that all?"

"I did the other ten on the train. I try to do all my homework on the day I get it, so all the rest of my homework for Monday is done."

Lavinia stared at Seb incredulously, her forehead wrinkled, then shook her head and went back to her books. Seb completed his questions and went to the living area at the other end of the room, where Uncle Matt and Aunt Karen were sitting on one of the sofas. Uncle Matt looked up from his newspaper. "Finished already?" he asked.

Seb nodded.

"Good," said Uncle Matt. He laid his paper aside. "Come with me. I need to go outside to check on a cow."

"Okay." He grabbed his coat from the office and put on his wellies. He followed Uncle Matt across the yard and into a shed. In a pen stood a large black cow.

"Mirabelle!" Seb laughed. "I'd forgotten that Vinnie had told me to wait and see."

At that moment, Mirabelle arched her back and bellowed a low, deep, earnest groan.

Seb watched, wide-eyed, then turned to Uncle Matt. "Is she calving?"

Uncle Matt smiled. "She is indeed! I think it'll be very soon now."

"Wow!" exclaimed Seb. To think that his favourite cow had chosen to calve the weekend he was at Cherryhill...

Seb leaned his arms on the gate and watched in amazement as two little white hooves appeared. Mirabelle shuffled her feet and pushed again. Soon, a black nose came into view, resting on the legs. Seb laughed. The calf had its tongue poking out the side of its mouth. He couldn't take his eyes off the miracle unfolding before him.

"She's doing well," commented Uncle Matt. "She's done this a couple of times before."

Once the head was out, it didn't take long for the calf to slide from Mirabelle's body. There it lay, wet and unmoving, on the straw. Uncle Matt pulled open the gate.

"Why isn't it moving? Is it okay?" asked Seb anxiously as he followed him into the pen.

"It'll breathe in a minute." Uncle Matt knelt beside the calf and rubbed his big hands over the mouth and nose, clearing away the clear, sticky mucus.

Suddenly, the calf gave a weak snort. It shook its head and large ears, then shuffled around on the straw. Uncle Matt lifted one of the back legs and smiled. "A heifer!"

Seb grinned. He'd been on the farm often enough to learn that a heifer calf meant a new cow for their herd someday or a more valuable animal to sell on. He figured Uncle Matt would want to keep Mirabelle's daughter and he was looking forward to seeing her grow up. He reached down to touch her. She was warm and slimy, steam rising from her gangly body. She blinked, confused. "You poor girl," Seb told her. "All warm and comfortable, then forced into this big, cold world. But don't worry; Cherryhill is a good place to live. There's nowhere like it."

When Uncle Matt finished checking Mirabelle, he and Seb washed their hands and wellies, then made their way to the house.

"A heifer!" Uncle Matt called, as they walked through the kitchen door.

His announcement was met by a cacophony of voices.

"Yippee!" Martha cried, bouncing up and down and waving her arms in the air.

"She's had it already? Why didn't you come and get me?" Lavinia threw down her pen and pushed back her chair.

Aunt Karen got up from her seat in the living area. "Oh, Matt! That's wonderful!" She wrapped her arms around her husband, heedless of the smells and questionable substances on his checked flannel shirt.

Seb watched the family as they discussed the birth and the new addition to Cherryhill, then closed his eyes as Uncle Matt thanked God for the safe arrival of the heifer calf and for the preservation of Mirabelle. Seb silently added his own prayer of thanks, for this family and for their love and care for him, and for letting him see the miracle of new life.

———

Seb pulled back the green blanket and quilt and climbed into bed. The house was quiet and the room dark. He'd forgotten how big the bed was. He stretched his arms wide and still couldn't reach the edges. Wouldn't it be wonderful if Mum could afford a bigger house, and, even better, one in the country? He could go to school with Lavinia, milk cows in the evening, help to train Glen, watch Mirabelle's daughter grow up... He sighed. A verse he'd read in the Bible a few weeks ago came to mind. He'd underlined it with a red pen. *I have learned in whatever state I am, to be content...*

Content. In a little house or in a big one. In the city or in the country. At school or on the farm. No matter the circumstances, difficult or easy, with God's help it was possible to be content. God had him in Belfast for a reason, and until He saw fit to change his circumstances, he would live for Him as best he could. Seb's thoughts drifted to Mum. He wondered how she was getting on. She wasn't working this weekend, and he'd tried to persuade her to come with him, but she'd declined. She wanted to paint his bedroom, she'd told him.

"It's not urgent, Mum. My bedroom will wait," he'd said.

She'd quickly shaken her head. "No, Seb, it's okay. You go and enjoy yourself. I'll be fine." He'd wondered at the look he saw in her eyes. She clearly didn't want to spend a whole weekend with Matt and Karen just yet. He often prayed for her; he knew she wouldn't have peace until she knew her sins forgiven and Christ as her Saviour. Whatever it was that she thought was unforgiveable, well, it didn't matter. God could forgive big sins as well as little sins, *if there really is such a thing*, thought Seb with a wry smile.

Seb yawned and adjusted his pillow. He was beginning to get really sleepy. The fresh country air was having an effect on him already. As he drifted off to sleep, he dreamed about a little black and white heifer calf, her large, friendly mother standing over her, watching her every move.

Chapter Twelve

"Seb! *Seb!*" a voice hissed outside his bedroom door. Seb's eyelids felt glued together as he forced them open. Where was he? Gradually, the room came into focus – the green curtains, the large, heavy wooden furniture. Cherryhill Farm.

"What is it?" he croaked, voice hoarse as he rubbed the sleep from his eyes. What time was it anyway?

"I'm going out to start the milking. I didn't think you'd want to miss it."

Seb sat up, instantly wide awake. "Okay, Vinnie," he called. "I'll be down right now."

He dressed quickly and made his way out into the fresh, cool morning. A mist hung in the air and he breathed deeply, inhaling the scent of farmyard and cows. Lavinia was waiting for him across the yard. "Hurry up, slowcoach!" she called, turning and making her way down the back lane.

Seb broke into a run, pausing to close the gate behind him. He slowed down when he caught up with his cousin. "Do you help with every milking now Joe's gone?" he asked. Joe had been the farmhand at Cherryhill before he was discovered helping to rustle cattle. During the summer, Seb, with the help of Lavinia and their friends, Caleb and Rebekah, had uncovered the identities of the men who had plagued the countryside, thieving cattle and smuggling them across the border. The plan hadn't gone smoothly, however, and Seb and Rebekah had ended up in a very dangerous situation. Joe had decided to risk the wrath of his fellow criminals to help rescue the young people and Seb hoped Joe would get a more lenient sentence because of the part he played. No matter how it went, his days in Northern Ireland were over – betraying his friends meant that if he stayed, he would be in danger.

"Only at weekends and in the evenings," replied Lavinia. "Caleb actually comes to help Dad during weekdays with the morning milking until he finds someone else. If things get busy around the farm, Tommy comes for an hour or two to help, but he's busy with his own farm and isn't getting any younger. A good farmhand with the sort of hours Dad needs help with is hard to find."

Seb laughed. "And you haven't persuaded your dad to let you help in the morning instead?" It was very obvious to everyone who observed them that Lavinia and Caleb were more than a little interested in each other.

Lavinia went red. "Well, that would hardly make sense!" she exclaimed. "Dad would have to do the evening milking by himself. That sort of defeats the purpose of getting someone to help!"

Seb chuckled. He loved teasing his cousin. She always got so wound up.

They reached the field where the cows were and Lavinia opened the gate to let them through. Apart from his initial fright, when Mirabelle managed to land him in the muck, he always enjoyed watching the magnificent animals striding past. Occasionally they stopped to regard him with big, intelligent eyes, then continued on their way.

———

After milking, when the last cow had left the parlour, Seb left Lavinia washing everything down with the pressure washer and headed to the calving pen. Mirabelle looked up as Seb approached, the calf standing on knobbly legs beside her. The baby was a miniature of her mother, right down to the shape of the white patch on her black head. The calf's coat had dried and she looked soft and fluffy, her large, black ears protruding from each side of her head. Uncle Matt had been here already this morning and a yellow eartag hung from each ear.

Mirabelle leaned down and licked the black fur, then looked back at Seb. She almost looked proud of her baby. "Isn't she cute?" she seemed to be asking.

"Oh, yes, very cute!" Seb nodded, then looked furtively around. He hoped no one had heard him having a conversation with a cow.

Seb didn't know how long he stood watching Mirabelle and her daughter, but soon his belly began to rumble. The noise of the pressure washer died away and Lavinia joined him.

"Isn't she great?!" she exclaimed. "I love this time of year when the cows are calving."

"I thought summer was the best time of year on the farm," Seb said, a teasing smile on his face.

Lavinia giggled. "I did say that, didn't I? Was that your first day here?"

Seb grinned. "Yes. I couldn't stand you at the start." He'd arrived at Cherryhill at the beginning of the summer with a deeply ingrained hatred of Christians but had been shocked to discover after a few weeks, that, while her parents were Christians, Lavinia had never actually put her trust in the Lord Jesus Christ for salvation. By the end of the summer they'd become very good friends and Seb often prayed that she would soon be saved.

"Ha!" Lavinia gave a short laugh. "The feeling was mutual, I can assure you!"

The cousins laughed and turned to walk back to the farmhouse. There was sure to be a delicious breakfast awaiting them.

———

After evening milking, Seb showered and changed into a fresh pair of jeans and a shirt and made his way downstairs. The table was extended to its full length and set for twelve. Aunt Karen was busy stirring something on the stove, a blue apron tied around her waist.

"Can I help?" Seb asked.

Aunt Karen looked round. "Oh, yes, Seb, that'd be great. Maybe you could stir this sauce for me. I don't want it to stick, but I need to get the dessert in the oven." She handed him the spoon and went outside to get cooking apples from the garage.

It wasn't long before Lavinia appeared in the kitchen. She walked over to Seb and peered into the saucepan. "Cheese sauce?" she asked.

"Looks like it," he said, then took a step back, bending over and coughing loudly. Lavinia turned her head to look at him and frowned. "What's wrong with you? Did you swallow a fly or something?"

Seb put a hand over his mouth and nose. "Did you run out of water for your bath?"

"What in the world are you talking about, Sebastian? Of course I bathed. And anyway, you're dripping cheese sauce on the floor."

Seb quickly returned his spoon to the saucepan and chose to ignore her use of the name he disliked so much. "I'm not saying you didn't bath. I'm just wondering if you used water or if the bath was filled with perfume."

Lavinia narrowed her eyes at him, but she blushed. "What's wrong with a girl wearing a little perfume?"

Seb threw back his head and laughed. "Nothing at all," he replied. "But that's not a little perfume; that's the whole bottle!"

The back door opened and Aunt Karen stepped back into the kitchen. She set the apples on the bench and walked over to the stove to check on the cheese sauce.

"Oh my, Lavinia!" she exclaimed. "I think you've overdone the Marc Jacobs, dear!"

Seb sniggered.

"I don't know what you're talking about," she lied, but she grabbed a tissue from her pocket and began to discreetly scrub at her wrists.

"I'm sure Caleb will appreciate the effort you've gone to," said Seb solemnly, bracing himself for attack.

"Well, you aren't exactly still smelling of cows yourself," Lavinia remarked. "Any reason for that?"

Seb smiled at his cousin. "Not everyone is in the Cow Aroma Appreciation Society, you know," he told her. "I don't think Mrs Harvey likes it very much."

"Huh!" replied Lavinia. "I hardly think you're too worried about Sarah Harvey. Maybe her daughter…"

"Okay, you two," Aunt Karen turned away from the bench, knife in one hand and apple in the other, "enough of that! No one is out to impress anyone, got it? Or at least they shouldn't be. You're both much too young."

Lavinia turned to Seb and rolled her eyes.

"Lavinia!" scolded Aunt Karen, unwittingly shaking the knife at her daughter. "I saw that! I've half a mind to send you to your room and not let you out until our guests have gone home."

Seb couldn't suppress the snort of laughter at the panic-stricken look on his cousin's face, but he quickly turned back to the cheese sauce when Aunt Karen's gaze came to rest on him.

———

The Harveys arrived promptly at 7:30pm. They all seemed genuinely pleased to see Seb again and he enjoyed the banter and laughter. When the last of the toffee apple pudding and custard had disappeared and the parents took their coffee into the formal sitting room, Seb caught Rebekah's eye. He'd been hoping to get a chance to talk to her on her own. Rebekah was a believer in the Lord Jesus Christ and it had been while she was quoting a verse that Seb had put his trust in Christ.

"Want to go see the new calf?" he murmured, as he set a pile of dirty bowls and spoons beside the sink.

She pointed to the pile of saucepans and various cooking utensils in the sink. "After these are done," she replied quietly, pushing up her sleeves and squirting washing-up liquid into the sink. Seb grabbed a tea towel and began to dry, while Caleb and Lavinia loaded the dishwasher.

As the last saucepan was dried and set into the cupboard, Lavinia spoke. "Hey, we should go out and see the new calf!"

Seb inwardly groaned. Once Lavinia decided on a course of action, everyone had to comply. He glanced at Rebekah and gave a sheepish shrug. She bit her lip, laughter in her blue eyes. *Wait and see*, she mouthed.

Seb frowned. Wait and see? What for?

The four young people made their way across the yard and into the shed. The day-old calf was looking more confident on her feet as she walked closer to the gate.

"Aw, she's beautiful!" exclaimed Rebekah as she crouched down and tried to encourage her to come closer. Seb watched as the calf took a nervous step and thrust her black nose into Rebekah's hand, then swiftly backed away. After a few trial runs, she licked Rebekah's hand. Rebekah giggled. "Their tongues are so rough!" she said, as the calf began to suck on her fingers.

She pulled her hand away and scratched its cheek instead. The calf shook her head and the eartags flapped back and forth.

Straightening up, Rebekah looked round. "Where did Caleb and Vinnie go?"

Seb glanced behind him and shrugged. "I'm not sure; I didn't see them leave."

Rebekah laughed. "I figured they'd sneak off somewhere. They're always using me as an excuse, then I either get left on my own or feel like a gooseberry."

Seb laughed. "Well, I'm not complaining!"

Rebekah smiled. "So, how have you been getting on back in Belfast?"

Seb paused before he answered. So much had happened since he'd gone back that he didn't know how to condense it. "Okay," he answered slowly. "There have been good things and bad things. Since I got saved, everything is so different to me. Things that are important aren't anymore, and things that I couldn't have cared less about are very important to me now."

"What sort of things?" asked Rebekah, as she grabbed a handful of straw and tried to rub the sticky calf saliva from her hand.

"Well, I've discovered I can't stand bullying, and my old friends now want nothing to do with me, which is fine, of course. I want to work at school now and do my best, even if my best isn't great."

"How did your friends react when you told them that you'd got saved?"

Seb gave a dry chuckle. "You'll never believe what happened in the first week..." He began to tell Rebekah about Edward, the bullying, his reaction, and the aftermath when his jacket sleeve was slashed. Her blue eyes grew wide. "Oh, Seb! Does trouble just follow you around?"

Seb laughed. "It sure seems like it sometimes! But the good thing was that I discovered that my neighbour is a Christian lady and she told me about a wee gathering of Christians right at the end of my street. Can you believe that, Rebekah?"

She laughed with delight. "Isn't that just so wonderful?!" she exclaimed. "It's just what I was praying for!"

"You were?" asked Seb, astounded that this tall, blonde, pretty girl would actually spend time asking God to look after Seb.

"Of course!" she said. "Now, tell me more about this guy from Malaysia. What does he believe?"

By the time Seb had finished telling Rebekah about Edward's Buddhist beliefs, and she had told him how school was going for her this year, it was getting cold. Caleb and Lavinia hadn't appeared back into the shed, so they made their way to the house.

As they stepped through the back door, they met Uncle Matt on his way out.

"Oh, there you are!" he said. "I was wondering where you'd got to. I was just going to check you were okay."

"We were looking at the calf," Seb told his uncle.

Uncle Matt smiled. "That calf is well looked at anyway. You must have memorised every inch of her by now!"

Seb glanced at Rebekah. She'd gone a delicate shade of pink and was pulling straw from the bottom of her navy and pink shoe.

"Are Caleb and Vinnie back yet?" asked Seb.

"Quite a while ago, actually," replied Uncle Matt, looking amused. "You were out there well over an hour."

Seb bit his lip. It hadn't seemed as long. "We were just talking," he explained.

Uncle Matt patted his shoulder. "That's fine, Seb. You've a lot to catch up on. No need to explain yourself to me."

The others didn't let them off so lightly. Entering the sitting room to a chorus of whistles and catcalls, Seb plonked himself down in the corner, while Rebekah squeezed herself between Lavinia and her younger sister, Faith.

Aunt Karen quickly took pity on the young people and grabbed a box of hymnbooks from the cupboard. She distributed them to everyone, then pulled out the piano stool and sat down. "Now," she said. "Anyone have a hymn they'd like to sing?" Seb knew what hymn he'd like, but he couldn't remember the first line in order to look it up in the index at the back.

"Aunt Karen, do you know the one that goes 'Because the sinless Saviour died...'?"

"Oh, yes, Seb. It begins 'Before the throne of God above'. That's a great hymn." She played an introduction and everyone began to sing.

As they sang, Seb's heart lifted in praise and worship to the God who had pardoned him through the death of His own Son, and who had brought him into the family of God. His own immediate earthly family might be somewhat dysfunctional, but his heavenly family, made up of people like Rebekah and Mrs Thompson, Uncle Matt and Aunt Karen… these were the people he would be in heaven with at the end of life. Heaven would be great. And most of all because the Lord Jesus Christ would be there, the One who had died for him.

Chapter Thirteen

"I'm sorry you can't stay longer," commented Aunt Karen over Sunday roast beef dinner.

"Me too," replied Seb. "The weekend has flown past."

"Well, maybe you can come and stay at half term," said Uncle Matt. "We've quite a few cows to calve around then."

Seb smiled. "I'd like that."

"Good!" exclaimed Lavinia, reaching for another potato. "It's all arranged. But maybe you can come before then. Half term is still ages away."

Uncle Matt chuckled. "We might have to talk to Seb's mum about half term first, Lavinia; Aunt Julie might have plans."

Lavinia raised an eyebrow at Seb and he shrugged. "Mum works a lot. I don't think she'll mind. But I'll ask her later."

"What was Madge saying to you this morning?" asked Lavinia. Madge and her brother, Tommy, were old neighbours and good friends of the McRoss family.

Seb laughed. "She was very offended that I was here and didn't go to see her. I promised her that the next time I came, I'd make a point of visiting. She was talking about her new pup. He sounds like a terror."

Everyone laughed. "He *is* a terror," said Uncle Matt, a twinkle in his eye. "You should have heard her telling about him grabbing her underwear off the washing line. Sweep thought it was great fun racing around the yard with Madge after him."

Lavinia giggled. "But the funniest part of the story is that the mineral man turned up in the middle of it and he managed to catch Sweep and extract Madge's underwear from him. Madge said she was 'clean affronted' when the mineral man handed her back her big frilly knickers!"

Seb set down his knife and fork and howled with laughter. He could clearly envisage the scene. "How on earth did you ever keep your face straight when she was telling you?" he finally sputtered.

Uncle Matt and Lavinia shook their heads. "We didn't! And Tommy was just as bad – apparently he just stood at the door while the whole drama was unfolding and chuckled away to himself. All three of us were in the bad books for a day or two!"

Seb smiled. There was never a dull moment when Madge was around. They finished their dinner and Lavinia cleared the plates away while Aunt Karen divided up the pudding.

"Rhubarb cobbler," she said as she set a bowl in front of Seb. "It's a new recipe, made with the last of the rhubarb. Help yourself to custard."

Seb poured a generous helping of custard onto the cobbler and dug in. "Mmm, delicious!" he said, mouth full of sweet, gooey cake and fruit.

"This is good, Karen," said Uncle Matt.

"I'm glad you both think so," she replied. "Now, I don't want to rush you, but you need to leave here soon if Seb's to catch the train."

Seb finished his dessert and drank a final glass of farm milk. He'd acquired a taste for the rich, unpasteurised milk over the summer and wished Mum could buy it in supermarkets in Belfast.

He took the stairs two at a time and began to pack. It didn't take long; his farming clothes stayed at Cherryhill, so he only needed to take home what he'd brought with him – his other clothes, pyjamas, socks and underwear, toothbrush, Bible, mobile phone and charger and his maths homework.

"All packed up?" asked Aunt Karen as Seb walked back into the kitchen.

Seb nodded.

"Good job," said Uncle Matt. "We'll take a moment to pray before we go."

Seb slipped back into his seat and closed his eyes as Uncle Matt thanked God for Seb's visit and asked Him to give Seb a safe journey home and help in the days ahead. "Amen," he finished.

"Amen," echoed Seb.

Aunt Karen, Lavinia and Martha stood on the doorstep and waved as Uncle Matt and Seb drove out of the yard. Seb hated leaving the farm and his family there, but God had placed him in Belfast and there he would stay for the foreseeable future. At least he was living with Mum; he really didn't know if he could survive if they were still living with Dad.

"So how are you getting on with that teacher?" Uncle Matt's voice broke through his musings.

"Mr Symons? My atheist biology teacher?"

"Yes, that's the one. I couldn't remember what you called him."

Seb sighed. "He just loves to make comments and nasty remarks about Christians. Sometimes there are things he says that I just don't have the answer for."

Uncle Matt slowed and then pulled out past a tractor which was crawling along the road. "Do you know something, Seb? Mr Symons doesn't have all the answers either. He might let on that he has his theories all watertight and no one can argue with him, but there are going to be some fundamental flaws in his reasoning. I had a lecturer at university like that, and it didn't matter what I said, he had an answer. There's not much point in a student arguing with a teacher on an intellectual level, but just remember that your God is the God who made the universe. He knows everything and Mr Symons doesn't, much as he might pretend he does."

"That's true," agreed Seb, "but do you think I should look into these things he's saying?"

"Absolutely, Seb," replied Uncle Matt. "You need to be informed about the topics from a creationist's standpoint as his interpretation is skewed to his viewpoint. In fact, one of the things which I am pretty sure he won't want to discuss in great depth is DNA. Have a look online when you get home and you'll see what I mean."

"Okay," Seb agreed. He was very grateful for Uncle Matt. At school, it was easy to feel that he was one little fish swimming against a great shoal of other fish, and knowing that there were others, also swimming against the current, gave Seb great encouragement.

At the station, Seb walked through the turnstile and around the corner, turning back once to wave at Uncle Matt. He felt a strange heaviness in the pit of his stomach. Nerves, he reckoned.

The train approached the station and Seb walked alongside until it had completely stopped. He waited until an elderly lady stepped down, then made his way on board. This time, there were plenty of seats, so he chose one at the window. The doors slid shut and the train moved off. He could see Uncle Matt's red jeep pulling out of the station. As the train took him farther and farther from his favourite place on earth, he began to be filled with a strange sense of foreboding. What was wrong? Why did he feel that things were about to change, that by the time he saw his uncle, aunt and cousins again, things wouldn't be the same?

———

Seb exited the doors of the station and glanced at his watch. 4:10pm. He had enough time to go home and have a snack and a chat with Mum before going round to Mrs Thompson's and walking with her to the Sunday evening service. She'd want to know all about his weekend at Cherryhill. Seb thought that perhaps Uncle Matt and his family reminded her a little of her own son and his family in London. He would have to make sure Mrs Thompson got to meet the McRoss family sometime. They'd get on well, he was sure.

He wondered if Mum would go with them tonight. She'd always been working when he went before. He really wished Mum was a Christian. He was worried about her. She had had a hard life; living with an abusive husband had taken its toll. So had the weight of guilt she was carrying around. Seb still had no clue as to what her secret was, but he was certain that it was nothing that the blood of Jesus Christ couldn't cleanse. What worried him most was that if anything happened to her, she wasn't ready to die. There had never been a time in her life when she had trusted Christ for salvation. If she died as she was, she wouldn't be in heaven, she'd be in hell. Seb shuddered. He could hardly cope with that thought. Asking God another time to save his mum, he hastened home through the busy Sunday afternoon Belfast streets.

Seb opened the door to the house and stepped inside. It wasn't like Mum to keep it unlocked, but she'd probably left it open for him coming home. He closed it behind him and turned the key. "Mum! I'm home!"

No response. The house was eerily quiet.

He dumped his bag at the foot of the stairs and pushed open the door to the living room. The curtains were drawn and the room was gloomy. A strange odour lingered in the air. Seb blinked as his eyes became accustomed to the semi-darkness.

He peered around the room. Furniture was out of place, pictures hanging at an angle, the TV knocked over. Something was wrong, terribly wrong...

Suddenly his eyes fell on a dark shape lying across the room at the kitchen door. He flipped the light switch and gasped at the sight, eyes wide with horror.

Crumpled on the floor, blonde hair matted and tangled, face battered and bruised, a pool of blood beside her head, was Mum.

Chapter Fourteen

"Mum! MUM!" Seb screamed, dashing across the room and crouching down beside the still, unresponsive form. Tears began to stream down his face as he grabbed her arm and shook it. "Mum! Wake up!" he wept. Had his worst nightmare really come true? Was she dead? He grabbed her wrist and searched for a pulse. Where was it? Why hadn't he paid more attention in health education classes when they were learning first aid instead of making crude jokes? "Oh, God! Help me!" he cried.

Suddenly, Mum moaned. She lifted a shaky hand. "Where am I?" she croaked.

Seb breathed a prayer of thanksgiving. She was alive!

"You're at home," he said. "What happened? How do you feel? Can you move?"

Mum turned her head a fraction to look at Seb through puffy, red lids. "Seb?"

"Yes, it's me. I just got home from Uncle Matt and Aunt Karen's." He reached into his pocket and pulled out his phone. "I'm going to call for an ambulance."

Mum struggled to sit up. Seb put a shaky hand on her shoulder.

"It's okay, just lie there." He dialled 999.

"No, Seb. You can't!" Mum's voice was full of alarm.

"Mum, you're hurt. How long have you been lying there?"

"Seb, don't phone!"

Seb ignored her pleas. He had a good idea who was to blame. But it was obvious she needed medical attention. Her left arm was badly swollen and blood trickled from a cut on her left cheek.

———

Seb went with Mum in the ambulance. He'd begun to protest when she told them she had fallen down the stairs, but one look at the face of the red-haired female paramedic told him that she didn't believe a word of the story. Why would she have fallen down the stairs and walked through the living room before she collapsed? They had likely seen plenty of domestic abuse cases anyway.

Mum stuck to her crazy version of events through doctors' examinations, through x-rays and scans and through getting her left arm in plaster. Halfway through, she added another false layer to her story – she had been drunk. At that, Seb's head swung round to look at her. He'd never known her to drink a drop of alcohol. She always claimed that it was the devil's brew and, after living with Dad, Seb was inclined to agree. The nurse noticed Seb's look of incredulity and narrowed her eyes. "Excuse me one moment," she said as she left the room.

A few moments later she returned with a package. *Help for victims of domestic abuse*, it read. Mum frowned. "I told you I was drunk and fell down the stairs," she told the nurse.

The nurse smiled at her. "Yes, you did," she acknowledged. "But why not take this anyway. You maybe know someone who could use the information."

Mum grabbed the package and set it face down under her chair. She looked exhausted and downcast, shoulders slumped, as if all life had been drained out of her.

Seb felt a slow rage beginning to build. How could Dad do this to her? And why? And how had he found her anyway?

After the examinations were complete, the doctor suggested keeping Mum in hospital overnight for observation. Mum point-blank refused.

"But, Mum, don't you think you ought to do as the doctor suggests? She's the expert, after all."

Mum shook her head wearily. "Seb, I've had enough. I just want to go home."

Seb shrugged helplessly and left the room to call a taxi to take them home.

———

As Mum stepped into the living room, she recoiled at the mess and the patch of blood on the carpet.

"Why don't you go up to bed and I'll bring you a cup of tea?" asked Seb, noticing her discomfort.

Mum bit her swollen lip and nodded, then turned and slowly climbed the stairs. Seb boiled the kettle and began to tidy the room. He didn't know what to do with the blood stain, so he lifted the mat from the back door and set it over it. Maybe Mrs Thompson would know how to remove it. He closed his eyes. Mrs Thompson! He had forgotten all about going with her to the service. He would need to visit her tomorrow to explain. Maybe she would stay with Mum while he was at school.

He dropped a teabag into a mug and filled it with boiling water. Lifting a teaspoon from the drawer, he stirred it around until the liquid was the right colour, then fished the bag out and dumped it in the sink. After adding a spot of milk and a big spoonful of sugar, he grabbed a packet of chocolate biscuits and headed upstairs.

Mum was sitting up in bed with the package the nurse gave her open beside her. Seb handed her the tea and set the biscuits on her bedside table, then reached for the bag of tablets she'd been given.

"One of these and one of these?" he asked, pointing at two different strips of blister packs.

Mum nodded and Seb pressed the tablets through the foil and handed them to her. She dropped them in her mouth and swallowed them down with a mouthful of tea.

He opened the biscuits and offered her the packet. Listlessly, she propped her mug between folds in the bedclothes, took one and began to nibble the edge.

"So, Mum. What *really* happened?"

Mum looked down at her tea. "You don't believe my story?"

Seb gave a short laugh. "Mum, I don't think *anyone* believed your story. It has more holes in it than a paper bag full of mice."

Mum sighed. She was quiet for a long time, sipping her tea and slowly eating the biscuit.

Finally, she spoke. "It was Alan." So, Seb was right. Dad had been here. He waited.

"I was watching TV and I heard someone at the door. I thought it was Mrs Thompson... but it wasn't." Mum shuddered. "He'd been drinking and he looked wild, worse than I've ever seen him before."

"Wow," said Seb flatly. "He must have been bad." They'd both seen Dad in his drunken rages.

Mum took another sip of tea. Her hand trembled. "I tried to close the door, but he stuck his foot in and forced it open. He... he hit me, and threw me around the room..." Mum's face crumpled and she began to weep. "He called me all sorts of names, told me I wasn't fit to live. I thought I was going to... to die."

Seb reached out and took the mug from Mum's hand. She was shaking violently. He set the tea on the bedside table and awkwardly rubbed her back. She was so small and frail. Softly, he began to pray.

Mum had no refuge from the storm, no shelter in which to hide. She wasn't ready to die and was afraid to meet God. She sobbed, a loud, keening wail, giving vent to the pent-up anguish and terror of years.

Finally, the crying subsided and she lay back, spent, on the bed. Seb stood up. "Get some sleep," he said. "Good night."

"Good night." Mum's voice was hoarse and soft.

Seb turned out the light and left the room. He padded softly downstairs and left the mug in the sink. He took one of the biscuits and poured himself a glass of milk, then went in search of his bag. Finding it on a coat peg at the front door, most likely hung there out of the way by one of the paramedics earlier, he reached in and retrieved his Bible. At the table, he opened the book. As he flicked through to find the place he had left off that morning, the beginning of one of the psalms caught his eye.

'God is our refuge and strength…' He paused. Today's happenings had been scary and disturbing. He needed to be reminded that God was still in control. He read on.

'God is our refuge and strength, a very present help in trouble. Therefore we will not fear, even though the earth be removed, and though the mountains be carried into the midst of the sea; though its waters roar and be troubled, though the mountains shake with its swelling. Selah… The Lord of hosts is with us; the God of Jacob is our refuge. Selah… Be still, and know that I am God; I will be exalted among the nations, I will be exalted in the earth!'

Seb reached for another biscuit. He tried to envisage what it would be like for the earth to have these disruptions. It would be like an earthquake, tsunami and volcano all happening at once. How terrifying! Yet, the writer said 'We will not fear'. Seb pondered the words. The only way that it was possible not to fear was to run to God, to be still – at rest – and remember that He is God. He is, and will always be, in control.

Seb took a deep breath. He didn't know what would happen in the days ahead. Now Dad knew where they lived, he could come back at any time. They would likely have to move again, leave this street and Mrs Thompson. But God said, 'Be still...' Seb wouldn't worry. God would look after him.

Finishing off the milk, he stood up and took the glass to the kitchen. The clock on the oven read 2:53. He yawned. It was going to be difficult to get up for school in the morning. Turning off the light, he left the room, double checked that the front door was locked and climbed the stairs to bed. It wasn't long before he was sound asleep.

———

An ear-piercing shriek split the air. Seb sat up in bed, heart pounding. What was wrong? He leaped out of bed.

"No! No! Please don't hit me!" It was Mum. Had Dad come back and broken into the house?

Seb ran to Mum's bedroom and opened the door. He wished he'd grabbed his phone on the way out of his room. The room was in darkness. He flipped on the light and raised his fists, ready to attack the intruder.

Mum sat up in bed, breathing hard, eyes bleary, hands trembling. She recoiled when she saw Seb standing, fists raised.

Seb glanced around the room. No one else was there. "Why were you screaming?" he asked.

"I'm sorry, Seb. I was having a bad dream. I thought he had come back." She shivered, the bruises standing out on her pale face. She reached for the bag of tablets. "Maybe one of these sleeping tablets will do the trick."

Seb helped her locate the tablet and brought a glass of water from the kitchen. She swallowed it and smiled bravely. "I'll be okay," she said. "Go back to bed."

"Are you sure?" Seb asked.

Mum nodded. "Um, Seb?" she said, as he turned to go.

"Yes?"

"Thank you. You're a good son. I don't know what I'd do without you."

As Seb walked back to his bedroom, he pondered Mum's words. He couldn't remember much praise growing up. Certainly none from his dad. And in the past few years he certainly hadn't done much to merit his mum's praise anyway. She had changed since leaving Dad – more independent, calmer, more in control. She had begun to poke her head out of the rabbit hole, instead of cowering inside. He hoped that this episode didn't send her scurrying back.

He crawled back into bed, but it was a long time before he dropped off to sleep.

Chapter Fifteen

Seb awoke with a jolt. He felt disorientated and confused. What had happened? Why did he have such an unsettled, almost nauseous feeling in his stomach?

Gradually the events of the previous day came tumbling into his brain. Coming home from Cherryhill. Mum. Ambulance. Hospital. Nightmares. He took a deep breath and rubbed his face. This must be Monday. So why hadn't the alarm gone off? Or had he wakened before his alarm?

He leaned over the edge of the bed and lifted his phone from the floor. Through bleary eyes, he stared at the screen and froze. Frowning, he blinked a few times. No way! 10:27am?

Seb leaped from the bed, yanking open the wardrobe and pulling out his school uniform. He hurriedly dressed, shoved his feet into his shoes and ran from the room. He took the stairs two at a time and barged into the living room. Mum was huddled beneath one of the pink throw blankets on the sofa. She jumped as he came into the room.

"Do you see the time?" he called as he raced past her and searched through the cupboards for something to eat. He pulled a couple of biscuits from the packet and shoved one in his mouth.

"Yes, Seb," said Mum weakly, as he ran past her on his way to the front door. "I thought you could take the day off. You were late to bed last night."

Seb grabbed his bag from the hook and stuck an arm through the strap. If he hurried, he could make it to chemistry class. Chemistry! Where were his books? He dropped the bag to the floor and opened it. Dirty underwear and socks jumbled up with his maths homework. He groaned and tipped everything on to the floor, then shoved his school supplies back. Jogging back upstairs, he pulled out his homework diary and piled up the appropriate books. The other books would be in his locker.

He was zipping his bag shut when he heard Mum calling from the living room. Her voice was still hoarse.

"What is it, Mum?" he asked, poking his head into the living room and once again hefting the bag on to his shoulder.

"Do you need to go to school today, Seb?" she asked.

"Mum, of course I need to go to school. If I miss classes I'll get way behind and it'll be even harder to catch up."

Mum took a deep breath. "Okay, you're right. Have a good day." She lifted her head and tried to smile through swollen, trembling lips. A tear glinted in her eye.

For the first time since he'd raced down the stairs, he stopped and looked at her. Her bruises were starting to darken. The cut on her left cheek was covered with a white plaster. Her nose looked as if it had been broken and she was cradling her white plaster-covered left arm. She looked a pitiful mess.

Seb dropped his bag. How selfish of him, thinking of nothing but himself, his education, his pride in working hard. He hung his bag back on the peg and returned to the living room. Today, there was something more important than schoolwork. Today, Mum needed him.

———

Seb was rummaging through the kitchen cupboards, hunting for lunch, when he heard a knock at the door.

"Seb!" Mum hissed. "Someone's out there!"

Seb went to the door.

"Don't open it. He might be back."

Seb paused, then ran upstairs instead and looked out Mum's bedroom window on to the pavement below. A white head. "It's okay, Mum. It's Mrs Thompson," Seb called, as he turned the key.

The neighbour was standing with a saucepan in her hands, a white plastic bag dangling from one wrist.

"Come in." Seb held the door open.

Mrs Thompson smiled. "I thought you could do with some soup today." She didn't seem to be surprised that Seb wasn't at school.

Neither did she look overly shocked at the sight of Mum, small and wounded, on the sofa. She set the pot and bag on the kitchen table and perched on the edge of the sofa, beside Mum.

"Julie, dear," she murmured, putting a white, wrinkled hand on Mum's back and rubbing it. "How are you? You look as if you've been through the war."

"I feel like it, too," Mum said with a faint smile.

"I'm sorry I wasn't here," Mrs Thompson went on. "I had been invited out to lunch and wasn't back home until later. I came round here to see you, Seb, but no one answered the door."

"We were likely at the hospital by then," Seb said.

"I was really worried when Herbert from across the street told me he'd seen you leaving in an ambulance. I'm glad you're at home. But your arm is broken?" asked Mrs Thompson.

Mum nodded, looking dejected. "I won't be able to work until the plaster comes off. It could be six weeks."

Mrs Thompson patted Mum's arm. "Well, how about some soup? I made it this morning – butternut squash. I've some bread as well."

"Sounds good, Mrs Thompson," said Seb, as he crossed the room and carried the saucepan into the kitchen.

————

Mum took tiny mouthfuls of her soup and nibbled at her bread.

Finally, she set down her spoon. "I'm sorry, Mrs Thompson. Your soup is delicious, but I'm just not hungry." Seb was alarmed. Mum hadn't eaten enough to keep a sparrow alive. She was already thin and pale and he hoped she would feel like eating more very soon.

"Don't worry, dear. I understand." Mrs Thompson smiled at Mum.

To Seb's surprise and horror, Mum glared at Mrs Thompson. "No!" she exclaimed. "I don't think you do! How could you possibly know what it's like to live for years with an abusive husband, to finally pluck up the courage to leave and then... then..." Mum began to sob.

Seb glanced at Mrs Thompson in alarm. What had got into Mum? Why was she attacking their sweet old neighbour like this?

"He insisted I let him in. He hit me! He swore at me. He threw me around the room. I thought I was going to die." Mum pushed her soup bowl away and buried her face in the crook of her arm. Her blonde, straggly hair hid her face as loud sobs filled the air.

Mrs Thompson stood up and began to rub Mum's back. "There, there," she murmured comfortingly. "You're right. I don't know what that's like." Gradually, the sobbing subsided and she persuaded her to go back to the sofa. Mum sat down and Mrs Thompson wrapped the pink blanket around her.

"You know," she began, as Seb cleared the table. Her voice was gentle, her tone conversational. "I don't know what it's like to live with a violent husband. Bobby was the most gentle man I ever knew. I've never faced violence at the hands of others, and I don't take that for granted. But did you ever hear of One who suffered much more violence? A completely innocent man. They beat Him, they spat on Him, they pulled His beard from His face, they hurled taunts and insults at Him, and when they had done all they could, they took Him and nailed Him to a cross of wood."

"Jesus Christ," whispered Mum.

"Yes," replied Mrs Thompson. "He hung on that cross for six hours and then laid down His life. And you know why He suffered and died? It was to save us from our sins. It was all for me! And for you, if you trust Him."

Mum sighed, her bony shoulders rising and falling. "I knew all about the crucifixion when I was growing up. I went to Sunday school, to church. I knew I needed to be saved." She paused, lost in another world, in another lifetime. Seb left the dishes. Something inside him told him this was crucial, that he should sit quietly and wait. He gently sat down on the kitchen chair he had vacated five minutes ago.

"My sister, Karen, got saved when she was eleven. I was twelve and I'd just started high school. I was making new friends, being introduced to people from backgrounds very different to ours. Karen changed. She wanted to read her Bible, to go to church. We grew apart."

Mum adjusted the sling supporting her plaster-clad left arm, then brushed strands of blonde hair from her face. She continued, "At sixteen I left school and began to attend college. One of the girls I met there became a good friend–" Mum broke off and gave a short, mirthless laugh. "I thought she was a friend, anyway. Her dad lived in Belfast and at the end of that year we decided to go and live there, get jobs. I left one evening. I didn't tell my family I was leaving. They came back from church and I was gone."

Seb listened. He'd heard this part of the story before, but he was no less shocked the second time round. He could hardly imagine just up and leaving a loving home, probably the type of home that Uncle Matt and Aunt Karen had. Had his mum been mad?

"The first week, my friend, Adele was her name, and I lived with her dad. He really didn't want two teenagers under his roof. We had to find somewhere else to live. One night, at a party, we met a bunch of university students. They were all a bit older than us, but they had a spare room that we could rent from them. It was a dingy, tiny space. We had to share a bathroom with everyone else." Mum shuddered. "I was there for two years. Many a night I wished I could go home, but I didn't want to face my parents. I got into all sorts of trouble. And those students treated us like slaves. We washed, cooked and cleaned for them to supplement the rent money."

Mum paused, staring into space. "Mum?" asked Seb.

She blinked and looked at him. It was almost as if she'd forgotten he was there.

"Didn't your parents ever come looking for you?"

Mum's face crumpled. She fumbled for a tissue. Mrs Thompson pressed a fresh linen hankie into her hand. "Yes," she replied. "Several times. It took them a long time to locate me. And when they did... " She took a deep breath.

"I was cleaning the bathroom. By this time, Adele decided she'd had enough and moved back to her dad's house. Cleaning the bathroom was my least favourite job, especially after everyone had had a big night out. Living with animals would have been much more preferable." She shuddered. "It was disgusting. A knock came to the door. I ignored it, hoping whoever it was would go away, but they persisted. Finally, I peeled off the rubber gloves and went to the door. I couldn't believe my eyes. There were Mum and Dad, standing with such a look of love in their eyes for me, their prodigal daughter. It's a wonder they recognised me at all – I was all dressed in black, my hair was dyed black and cut short and I wore heavy black makeup."

Seb tried to imagine his mum the way she was describing herself. He couldn't. He'd never seen any old photos around the house either.

"I was angry that they'd found me. I couldn't stand their love. They didn't know the things I'd done, the places I'd been. All they said to me was, 'Julie, we love you. Please come home.' And I...I... "

The tears began to stream down Mum's face. She blew her nose and carried on. "I told them to go away. That I hated them. That I never wanted to see them again."

Seb looked at Mrs Thompson. She was sitting calmly beside Mum. Her hands were clasped together and resting on her aproned knee. She had a very slight smile on her face, as if she was expecting good things to happen. Seb didn't quite understand. Mum's story was difficult to listen to and even more difficult for her to tell. She seemed to need to get it out. Maybe once she did that, she could move on.

Mum took a deep breath. "That was the last time I ever saw them." She sniffed and straightened her shoulders. "Shortly after that, I met Alan. I saw him as an escape route from the terrible house I was living in, from the thoughts that plagued me day and night. I threw myself into parties, into having fun, into anything and everything to stop me thinking about home and family and God. Alan was very possessive; he wouldn't let me out of his sight, and I think that's why he wanted to get married. After a while, Seb, you came along. And, well, that changed everything for me.

"I realised that I was now a mother, and I had to look after this baby. I stopped going to parties and stayed at home. I even tried to teach you Bible verses, Seb."

Seb's eyes widened. So that's why some of the verses he'd heard when he was at Cherryhill sounded familiar!

"Alan continued to party, and got increasingly angry when I refused to go with him. He wanted me to leave you with a neighbour. Then, when you got a bit older, I suggested sending you to Sunday school." Mum shuddered, sorrow etched deeply on every line on her face. "It was like lighting a fireworks warehouse. He'd been verbally abusive over the years, but that was the first time he got violent."

"What about your parents?" asked Seb quietly.

"I'm not sure how, but Karen eventually found my address. One day, she wrote to me, telling me that shortly after their visit to see me, Dad had taken a massive heart attack and died. Then, within a year, Mum had died from cancer. It was my fault," Mum sobbed. "If I had gone home, they likely would have been around today. And my last words to them were that I hated them." She broke down in tears. Mrs Thompson put her arms around her.

Seb felt like weeping too. His grandparents! He'd never known them. Getting up from the seat, he walked over and knelt before his mum. Now he knew why she kept insisting that it was too late for her to be saved. Her story was tragic. She couldn't undo the past, no matter how much she regretted it. But she could have a brighter future.

"Mum," Seb said earnestly.

She lifted her blotchy, bruised face and looked at him through her tears.

"Mum, the blood of Jesus Christ His Son cleanses from *all* sin. *All sin!*"

A faint glimmer of hope sparked in her eyes, then died away. She shook her head. "No. I rejected Christ. There's no hope for me."

"Mum, the Bible says *all* sin."

She looked at him for a long moment. Finally, "I'm tired," she said, struggling to stand. "I think I'll go to bed."

Seb felt like holding her back. He could see the battle for her soul and was afraid. Afraid that she would reject Christ again. Afraid that she would refuse to believe the truth. Afraid that the next time Dad saw her, he would kill her.

As she walked up the stairs, Seb sank onto the floor.

"Seb," Mrs Thompson spoke. He'd almost forgotten she was in the room. "God is working with your mother. She's never told you her story before and the telling of it has exhausted her. Give her a little time. Now," Mrs Thompson got off the sofa and slowly lowered herself to her knees, "let's pray. God is still in the business of saving souls."

Chapter Sixteen

Seb lifted his copy of Romeo and Juliet and a refill pad from his bag, then grabbed a pen. He might as well make a start on the English essay for Friday. He had barely written the title when he heard footsteps on the stairs, and the door to the living room opened.

"Did you have a good sleep?" asked Seb, without lifting his head.

There was silence. Puzzled, Seb looked around.

Mum was standing, still dressed in her pyjamas and dressing gown, hair still hanging in tangled strands. Despite her unkempt appearance and bruised and battered face, she was radiant.

"Oh, Seb!" she cried, as she ran towards him. Leaning down, she gave him a one-armed hug.

Seb was astounded. What had happened? Had she…? Was she…?

"Mum, what is it?" he asked.

"Seb, I got saved! Right there, in my bedroom." She pointed at the ceiling. "Oh, it's wonderful! The burden is gone. You were right; the blood of Jesus Christ does cleanse from all sin! I'm forgiven!"

Seb sat back in his seat and watched Mum. He had never seen her so happy before. The careworn look was gone, replaced by a peace that could only come from God. Joy flooded Seb's soul and his smile stretched wide as the realisation, that God had answered his prayer, dawned and grew. Mum now had a true Friend, One who would be with her every minute of every day, One who would lead her and guide her, and when the end of life came, whether next week or in fifty years' time, she would be in heaven.

Seb didn't manage to finish his essay that day. Who cared about essays when Mum had become a Christian? Even the angels in heaven rejoiced over sinners who repented.

———

That evening, they sat with a cup of tea and a slice of the carrot cake Mrs Thompson had brought over earlier. Mum had picked up the pack they had given her at the hospital and was flicking through the leaflets inside.

"I'm not sure it's wise to stay here, Seb," she said. During the day, the outward joy had been gradually exchanged for peaceful acceptance of her situation.

Seb slowly nodded. He knew she was right. "How did Dad find out where we live?"

Mum frowned. "I've no idea. For all we know, one of his 'mates', as he calls them, maybe lives in the area."

Seb looked down. "Actually...a green car followed me part of the way home from school. Looking back, I think it must have been him. I thought I'd shaken him off, but I guess I led him to the area." He looked at Mum's bruised face. "I'm sorry."

"Don't worry, Seb," Mum reassured him. "If he hadn't followed you, he'd have followed me. In fact, he likely waited around the place where he last saw you and followed me the rest of the way. I can't remember seeing a green car, but I was a bit preoccupied on Friday evening. He knew exactly where to come yesterday anyway."

Mum was right. Now that Dad knew where they lived, he could come back at any time. And if he got wind of the fact that Mum was now a Christian, the next time he paid a visit, she would be dead. All the same, Seb hated the thought of leaving here, of moving yet again. "Where would we go?" he asked.

Mum shrugged. "I really don't know, Seb. I signed a six-month contract on this house and it's nowhere near up yet. And I won't be earning for a few weeks, either." She paused, then handed Seb a leaflet from the package. "I was wondering about this."

Seb took the yellow pamphlet. *Safe accommodation*, it read. He opened it and flicked through the pages. "You think this is where we should go?" he asked. It seemed a little extreme. He knew Mum was in danger from Dad, but... "Can't we go and live with someone?"

"Who do you suggest?" she asked.

"Well, there's always Mrs Thompson," began Seb.

"Way too close. That would never work. And she's going to London soon to visit her son and family."

"Is she? I didn't know that."

"I think it was a spur of the moment thing. She'll be away for a month."

He'd no doubt that the people he knew from the Bible study and prayer meetings would gladly open their homes, but they also lived too close. "Well then, there's always Cherryhill. Uncle Matt and Aunt Karen would definitely take us and it's far enough away." For a moment, Seb allowed himself to dream. Wouldn't it be wonderful if they could move there?

Mum was shaking her head. "That's the most obvious place to look. I know it's not in Belfast, but that wouldn't stop your dad going there, and I don't want to put them in danger."

Seb bit his lip and began to list all the people he knew. Most of them were acquaintances of Dad's. Edward's family? He didn't know them well enough, and they had enough of their own problems without being asked to provide shelter for a victim of domestic violence.

"Seb, I'm going to phone the helpline," said Mum. "I think it's the right thing to do. No matter who we might think to ask, I'd be putting them in danger. If Dad found us here, he'd find us somewhere else too." She pulled the leaflet from his hand and looked around for her mobile. Finally locating it between two cushions on the sofa, she dialled the number.

Seb stepped out of the room and went upstairs. He didn't really want to hear Mum's side of the conversation. He flopped onto his bed. Why did Dad have to spoil everything for them yet again? Not for the first time, he wished that Dad wasn't really his dad after all.

Soon he heard Mum climbing the stairs. She rapped softly on his door and poked her head in. "Can I come in?"

Seb pushed himself up and leaned his back against the wall.

Mum looked nervous.

"What is it? Have they space?"

"Yes and no," she replied.

Seb frowned. "What do you mean?"

"They have room at one of their shelters, but only for me."

"What are you going to do?" Surely Mum wasn't going to go and leave him to fend for himself.

"I can either turn it down, or take it and find somewhere else for you to stay. It would be easier to find someone for you to stay with on your own. I'm the bigger risk."

Seb looked down. He secretly wished Mum would choose to turn it down, but he realised that wasn't really fair. Dad had proven that he was dangerous and Mum needed to be safe. "Take it," he said, lifting his head.

"Are you sure?" she asked. "I hate the thought of going there without you..."

"Take it," Seb repeated. "I'll be fine."

Mum nodded slowly. "All right," she said, and stood up. "I'll phone them now."

———

Seb stuffed his clothes into yet another black bin liner. Mum had got rid of the boxes she'd used when she'd moved here. He didn't know where all the contents of the house were going to go – Mum couldn't take everything to the safe accommodation, and Mrs Thompson could only store so much. Mum was leaving in a couple of hours. The helpline had advised her not to spend another night in the house. Mrs Thompson had kindly offered the use of her spare room to Seb until they could find somewhere safer and more permanent for him.

Picking up his schoolbooks, he shoved as many as would fit into his schoolbag and dropped the rest into another bin liner. The sharp edge of the biology textbook tore the bag down the side. Seb sighed and shook open another bag.

Finally, a row of stuffed black bags lay against the wall. All Seb's personal belongings were out of sight. The doorbell rang.

"It's the taxi," called Mum from her bedroom at the front of the house. "Grab one of these bags and tell her I'll be down in a minute."

Seb lifted one of the black bin bags from the door of her room and hefted it down the stairs. He opened the door. A lady was standing on the pavement outside.

Seb handed her the bag, and returned for another. Finally the bags were stowed in the boot and Mum came slowly down the stairs. She had dressed simply in a pair of black trousers and a blue sweatshirt. Her bruises were darker, but the swelling was beginning to reduce around her eyes.

"I love you, Seb," she said as she gave him a one-armed hug. "Be careful. I'll be in touch."

She stepped out the door and made her way to the car.

"Mum!" Seb called.

She paused. "What is it?"

"Do you have a Bible?" he asked.

Mum looked sad. "I used to…"

"Wait a minute!" he called, as he dashed upstairs. Retrieving his own Bible from his schoolbag, he returned to the front door. "Take mine," he said, as he handed it to her. "I can get another one."

Mum looked at him gratefully. "Thank you, son," she said. "I'm only borrowing it. When I get my own, I'll give it back."

Seb waved as the car drove off. He felt very alone. And yet, he wasn't alone. A verse he had read once came into his mind. 'When my father and my mother forsake me, then the Lord will take care of me.' And while his mum hadn't really forsaken him as such, it still held true that the Lord would take care of him.

He heard a door open and looked to his right. Mrs Thompson's snowy head peeped out. "Is your Mum gone already?" she asked.

Seb nodded.

"Oh dear," she tutted. "I was going to give her a Bible and some cookies."

"I gave her my Bible," Seb told her.

Mrs Thompson's eyes lit up. "That's great, Seb. You can have this Bible until you see her again. I'm sure the other Bible is quite special to you."

Seb nodded. "It was a present from Uncle Matt and Aunt Karen. I didn't appreciate it at the time, though." He laughed.

"But now it's your dearest treasure. Now, where are your belongings?"

————

Seb couldn't help but overhear the conversation going on downstairs. It seemed as if Mrs Thompson was trying to bypass the phone altogether.

"YES, JIMMY?!" she shouted. "IT'S ME, BETSY THOMPSON... I'M WELL, HOW ABOUT YOURSELF?...THAT'S GOOD, THAT'S GOOD... I'LL TELL YOU WHAT IT IS I'M PHONING ABOUT. I HAVE A YOUNG MAN HERE, HIS MOTHER HAS HAD A MISHAP AND HE NEEDS A PLACE...'

Seb stuck his head under the white embroidered pillow and pressed it to his ears. It muffled the words enough. He didn't really want to hear what Mrs Thompson had to say about him and his mum.

Soon the shouting ended and she came up the stairs. Footsteps stopped outside his room. "Seb?"

Seb opened the door.

Mrs Thompson's eyes were bright and she was smiling. "I've got good news for you. I phoned Jimmy and Edith. Jimmy's a distant cousin and they were neighbours of mine way back. They're able to keep you for as long as you need to stay. They live in a different area, so it's far enough away from here, but still close enough so that you won't need to change schools." She looked proud of herself.

Seb tried to mask the apprehension he felt. He didn't know these people. He wished he could just go to Cherryhill, but although Mum was longing to tell them she'd got saved, she hadn't felt ready to tell Matt and Karen about her ordeal just yet. And anyway, he would have to change schools. He knew, from what Lavinia had told him, that her school was usually oversubscribed and there was a good chance they wouldn't accept him, especially with his previous bad behaviour. It was a lot easier to stay at his current school at least until the end of this term.

———

The taxi drove slowly along the street. Mrs Thompson was sitting beside Seb, and all his belongings, still in the bin liners, were in the boot. School hadn't gone well today. He'd felt out of his depth with having missed the previous day, not helped by the fact that they had moved on to a new topic in maths. He hoped Jimmy and Edith didn't live too far from Edward; he could do with his assistance again.

Seb glanced behind him as the taxi turned left at the end of the street. Mrs Thompson saw his wistful gaze. "Don't worry, Seb. You can still come and visit."

Seb smiled at her. He was very thankful for the sweet old lady, her encouragement and her treats. He hoped Edith was half as good a baker, at least.

"You know what I was reading this morning?" Mrs Thompson didn't wait for an answer. "I was reading in Exodus about the children of Israel. You know the story, how they were in bondage in Egypt. They cried out to God and I'm sure it seemed to them at times that He didn't hear them or even care. But God said to Moses, 'I have seen the oppression, I have heard their cry, I know their sorrows.' Then He tells them He has come down to deliver them. Don't you think it's wonderful, Seb, that God sees, hears, and knows…and delivers?!"

Seb smiled. It was just the reminder he needed. His prayer was that things wouldn't always be like this – unstable and unsettled. Someday he and Mum would have a home where they would be safe, where Dad couldn't hurt them.

He glanced out the window and frowned. A slow realisation was dawning on him. "Mrs Thompson, are we almost there?"

Mrs Thompson leaned past the headrest of the front passenger's seat. "Yes, Seb, I do believe we are."

The taxi turned the corner and pulled to a stop. "Here we are," called the large, grey-moustached driver.

Seb felt sick. He knew this area. It was somewhere he'd hoped never to live again. Deliverance? This was like stepping back into bondage.

They were just around the corner from Dad's house.

Chapter Seventeen

The taxi bearing Mrs Thompson pulled away from the kerb. Jimmy and Edith stood beside Seb and waved vigorously until it turned the corner and disappeared from sight. Then they turned to Seb.

"Right, young man!" exclaimed Jimmy. "Let's go inside and we'll show you your room."

Seb picked up his schoolbag from just inside the front door and followed the old couple as they slowly made their way up the stairs. Jimmy clung to the handrail with both hands and took the steps one at a time. "These old knees…" he said.

At the top, Edith stopped and took a few deep breaths, then opened the door to the left. "Here you go," she said. "There isn't much room, but it's all we have."

A small, single bed was pushed against the wall. The room also held a chest of drawers piled high with boxes and miscellaneous household items. An ironing board and a clothes horse rested against the wall, and the plastic pipe of a vacuum cleaner protruded from under the bed. There looked to be barely room for Seb, never mind his belongings downstairs in the bin liners. But, still…

"Thank you very much," he told the old couple. Jimmy beamed. Edith nodded curtly.

"The bathroom is over there." Edith pointed to the door at the top of the stairs. "Oh, you'll probably need a towel." She pulled open another door and poked around inside the airing cupboard, finally emerging with a light brown towel. She handed it to Seb. It felt rough, as if it had been around for many years and dried bone-dry on the washing line.

"I'll make a start on dinner. You probably have homework to do." With that, the old pair made their way slowly back downstairs.

Seb stepped into the tiny, cluttered room and shut the door. He lowered himself onto the bed. It squeaked violently and sagged. He was getting really fed up moving around from house to house, and this was the worst scenario yet. He was wondering if he should have said to Mrs Thompson that Dad lived near here, but she'd been so pleased about finding him somewhere to stay and so excited about her upcoming trip to London that he hadn't wanted to burst her bubble. He would just have to be extra careful and try to avoid meeting Dad.

Seb tried to do his homework on the bed, but the mattress was so saggy that his writing was unreadable. Transferring the books to the floor, he leaned on one elbow. He could hardly face the thought of battling through the quickly-accumulating list. He was tempted to forget about it – he had rarely done homework last year, and it hadn't brought any severe consequences. Surely it wouldn't matter if he closed his books and took the evening off. Didn't he deserve it? He'd been through a lot these past few days.

Whatever you do in word or deed, do all in the name of the Lord Jesus...

Seb sighed. He certainly didn't feel like it, but he was pretty sure the verse included homework. Bending over his book again, he lifted his pen.

———

Sunlight streamed through the window. Seb yawned and stretched. Another morning, another bed in which to wake up. He could hear the sound of a radio blaring somewhere in the house. The bed tipped to one side as he swung his legs over the edge. Grabbing the hard brown towel, he made his way across the hallway to the bathroom.

Fifteen minutes later, having showered with a strange-smelling body wash, he made his way downstairs for breakfast. Edith was sitting in an armchair at the window, a small, hard-backed book in her hands, while Jimmy was standing at one end of the kitchen table, working on what appeared to be an old radio. Tools and radio parts of every size and shape were spread out before him. The couple looked up as Seb entered the room.

"Well, young man," said Jimmy, looking up from his work. "Sleep well?"

"Not bad," Seb said. He didn't want to tell them that he had tossed and turned for a long time, trying to find a position where a mattress spring wasn't digging into his side.

"It always takes me a night or two to get used to a new bed," commented Edith, her finger marking her place. "Are you ready for breakfast?"

Seb nodded.

"Well, just go ahead and help yourself. There's bread beside the toaster and some jam in the fridge. I'm afraid we don't have much in the way of cereal. And I hope you don't want a cooked breakfast." She peered at him over her plastic-rimmed spectacles.

"Toast is fine," he replied quickly. He wasn't going to get spoiled here, that was for sure. Locating the bread, he dropped two slices into the toaster and found the butter and jam. Clean mugs and plates were piled onto the draining rack, so he extracted one of each and filled the mug with milk.

He carried his breakfast into the living room and hesitated. The table was still cluttered. Choosing the other armchair, he sat down and silently gave thanks for his food. As he lifted his head, he noticed Edith frown.

"Did you use butter *and* jam?"

Seb looked guiltily down at his toast and back at Edith.

"It's butter or jam. Not both. And do you drink milk?" she demanded before he had a chance to apologise for his unwitting misdemeanour.

"Yes," he replied uncertainly.

Edith pressed her lips together. "Mm. I'll need to buy more. I thought we had enough to last us until the weekend, but if you drink milk then we obviously don't."

"I'm sorry, Edith. I can drink tea from now on."

She waved a hand dismissively. "I suppose growing boys need the goodness in milk."

"Yes, Edith, of course they do!" exclaimed Jimmy. "It's not as if we have to travel to Dublin to buy it." He grinned at Seb as he lifted a screwdriver.

Seb was quite relieved to finish his breakfast. He left his plate and mug in the sink and turned to go upstairs.

"Aren't you going to wash your dishes?" asked Edith, indignantly.

Seb froze, then spun around. "Sorry." He retreated to the kitchen.

Finally, back in his bedroom, he lifted the Bible Mrs Thompson had given him and began to read. He didn't have very long and he found it difficult to concentrate. He felt an unsettled feeling, but couldn't decide whether it was due to being in this area, so close to Dad, or living with people he barely knew. Maybe a combination. He shut his Bible and stood up. It was time to leave anyway.

———

Seb breathed a sigh of relief when he walked through the front doors of the school. He had avoided Dad's street and had made it without catching sight of him at all. He was still quite early, but he made his way to the biology classroom which doubled as his form room. Edward was already in his assigned seat for biology, the first class of the day, a book in his hands. Seb didn't feel like conversation, so he gave him a wave and headed for his own seat in the back corner of the room.

Mr Symons marched into the room and slammed his briefcase on the desk at the front. He looked to be in a really foul mood. Seb sighed. When Mr Symons was in a bad mood, Christians became the target for his anger.

"Quiet!" yelled Mr Symons from the front of the room after he had called the roll. "Get out your books."

The noise died away somewhat, replaced by the unzipping of schoolbags and the rustling of pages.

"Now, open up your books to chapter seven. We're going to move on to the next topic."

Seb frowned. They weren't due to finish the current topic until half term.

"Problem, Mitchelson?" Mr Symons was glaring at him.

"No, sir," replied Seb, quickly turning to chapter seven. *Introduction to evolution.* He groaned.

"Good. I thought you were going to argue against science, for a minute. You know the way you've become a *Christian!*" he spat.

Seb ducked his head and rummaged for a pen. When he glanced up, Mr Symons had turned away.

"Now, who can tell me whose name is usually associated with the theory of evolution?"

"Darwin," answered Zoe.

"Yes," replied Mr Symons. "He wrote a book in 1859 detailing his theory of evolution. But not everyone was convinced. And," he glared at Seb and lowered his voice, "not everyone is convinced nowadays as well. Some people think that *God* made the world. God! Nothing but a figment of the imagination." He gave a sardonic grin. "There is no God!"

Seb's heart sank. When Mr Symons got started on an anti-God spiel, nothing could calm him down.

"We don't need a God to tell us what to do! We don't need a God to threaten us into doing good! We aren't specially 'created' – we are here by pure chance." Mr Symons paced backwards and forwards across the room, clenched fist punctuating each point he was making. "All religion is poisonous and the sooner we eliminate it, the better!"

Poisonous? All religion? Seb watched Mr Symons pacing the room, a look of scorn twisting the teacher's features. Why did he think all religion was poisonous?

"Now," he took a deep breath and continued in a calmer voice, "we see that the first life forms developed over three billion years ago. These are called prokaryotes. Then we had eukaryotes…"

Seb looked down at his textbook. The picture of a pile of small, grey, bullet-shaped cells blurred. He knew Mr Symons wasn't right. Seb was convinced that God made the world, the plants, animals and human beings. It didn't come into existence by a big bang, and life on earth did not evolve from these little simple cells on the page before him. But Mr Symons' confidence was unsettling. While Seb knew he was right, he felt stupid and unlearned.

"Did you agree with that, Mitchelson?"

Seb jumped. He didn't know what Mr Symons had just said, but whatever it was, he was pretty sure he didn't agree at all.

Mr Symons walked over to Seb and leaned his hands on the table in front of him. "Do you agree that we are here because of evolution?"

Seb took a deep breath and straightened his shoulders. "No, sir."

Mr Symons stood up and slapped a hand on the table. "You fool!" he sneered. "Give me one reason why you don't think evolution happened."

Seb scrambled for an answer. The contempt in Mr Symons' eyes had driven all reasonable thought from his head.

"There you go! You can't even think of one!"

Seb dropped his head and groaned. This day hadn't started off very well. Surely it could only improve. And where on earth had it all gone wrong? As Mr Symons continued to discuss the theory of evolution, Seb cast his mind back over the morning from the moment he got up. He mentally walked through the day…and paused. His Bible reading! He'd only glanced at the Bible that morning, *and didn't pray*, he thought sadly. How could he have expected the day to go well if he hadn't taken the time to pray. Quickly bowing his head, he confessed his sin to God.

As he looked back at the textbook, a memory came to mind. Uncle Matt, in the jeep on the way to the train station. They'd been discussing Mr Symons and his attitude towards Christianity. What was it he had told him to look up, that evolution struggled to explain? Seb absentmindedly flicked through the textbook. A brightly-coloured double helix caught his eye. DNA! He didn't know very much about DNA, but he soon would know a lot more about it than he did now. The bell rang and he closed the book and put it into his bag. The next time Mr Symons asked him a question like that, he'd be prepared.

Chapter Eighteen

"Excuse me, we're closing in fifteen minutes." Seb looked up from his English essay to see a young, pink-haired librarian standing beside his desk.

Seb nodded politely and she moved on. Typing the last few words of his essay, he saved it and logged off. He packed his books away, then stood up and made his way outside into the September evening. Coming to the library had been a good idea. Unable to face the thought of going back to Jimmy and Edith's to do his homework on the bedroom floor, he had decided to make use of the local library. He could envisage spending a lot more time here over the next few weeks.

Another advantage of the library was the free Wi-Fi. He had made a good start on researching DNA and had found a lot of very interesting information. He'd already learned in school that DNA molecules carry a genetic code, and this code determines the characteristics of a living organism. What he hadn't realised was that DNA held so much information – each human has about three billion pairs of chemical letters, and information in a trillion books could be contained in a pinhead-sized sample of DNA. It made his mind spin to consider that very tiny differences could make huge changes. How did evolutionists ever think that this could have evolved in such a way as to produce all the amazing features and characteristics in both human beings and animals? Wasn't it much more sensible to admit that, in the same way that a computer program must have been created by a software engineer, so DNA must have been designed by a Creator?

Seb stopped at the footpath and looked both ways before crossing the street. He'd been very interested to read of a former atheist who had been so convinced of the language-like code of DNA, among other things, that he had changed his mind about the existence of a Creator. Of course, atheists liked to write him off as an old man who'd lost his marbles, but Seb thought that if the rest were as honest, they might actually change their minds too.

Seb's stomach rumbled. He wondered if Edith would have made the dinner, or if she would expect him to fend for himself. She was certainly a gruff old lady and Seb couldn't quite work out if she was all noise, or if she really didn't appreciate a teenage guest in their house. He'd have to tread carefully and try not to offend her. Jimmy was different, he…

A blare of a car horn jolted him from his thoughts. He glanced around to see whose attention the driver was trying to attract and froze in horror. The green Ford Focus with the heavyset figure of his dad in the driver's seat was pulling alongside the kerb. He hoisted his schoolbag more securely on his back and prepared to run.

"Hey, Seb!" called his dad. He actually sounded... friendly? Was that even possible? Seb hesitated. "Come over here; I want to talk to you."

Seb walked slowly over to the car. He stopped far enough away so that he could still turn and run if his dad decided to go after him. He looked calm and reasonable today, though. "What is it?"

"I just want to know where your mum is. I want to apologise."

Seb narrowed his eyes at Dad. He didn't believe that story for a minute.

"Honest, Seb. I'm really sorry for what I did."

"How do you know you didn't kill her?" he asked, rage building up inside him.

"Ah, come on! You know I'm not a murderer," replied Dad. "She said something that made me mad and I couldn't help myself. Where did she go?"

"I don't know, and even if I did, I wouldn't tell you."

"Bet you she's in one of those shelter places. But where are you staying?"

"With friends." He hoped that calling Jimmy and Edith 'friends' wasn't stretching the truth too badly.

"Near here?"

Seb shrugged. He didn't want to give Dad any more details,

neither did he want to lie.

"Well, you're my son. You ought to live with me. I'll be contacting social services and arranging to get custody of you. Of course," he paused and rubbed a hand over his stubbly double chin, "that'll mean trying to find your ma. She'll not give you up in a hurry, so she might need to be persuaded."

Seb took a deep breath. 'Persuaded' was Dad's word for 'threatened'. But surely he would never find her.

"There can't be many of those shelter places," he murmured, gazing out the windscreen of the car, "and I have friends who could help. If that fails, well, I'm sure she can't be locked inside all the time…"

Seb felt trapped. Dad was right. He likely would find her somehow. Why hadn't he just run away when he saw Dad's car?

"Or," his dad continued, shrewdly, "you could save me any hassle and just come home to my house again. I got a new TV since you last lived there. A big one! You'll love it." He seemed to have forgotten that Seb had paid a visit to find his PE kit.

"I'll-I'll think about it," replied Seb, taking a step back from the car.

Dad fixed Seb with a hard gaze. "I wouldn't think too long about it, if I were you," he said. "You have until eight o'clock to get back under my roof."

Seb gulped. Dad obviously meant business.

Dad started the car again and revved off. The nearest wall happened to be a gable wall of a row of terraced houses and Seb staggered across and leaned against it. *Life would be so much more straightforward without Dad*, he thought, then grimaced. He didn't want his dad to die; he knew for sure that he would be in hell. In his mind, he knew that Christ died so that all could be saved, even Dad, but the idea that atheistic, bitter Dad could ever become a Christian was too much for Seb to imagine. He usually prayed for Dad, but in a half-hearted and disbelieving way. Could God really save someone like him?

Seb pushed himself upright and slowly continued on his way to Jimmy and Edith's. As he walked, a verse that he had read and underlined bounced into his mind.

'For with God nothing will be impossible.'

Really? Even Dad's salvation? He bit his lip. He had actually been doubting God!

He pushed open Jimmy and Edith's front door. The smell of food frying hit his nostrils and, despite his encounter with Dad, his stomach growled. Entering the living area, he saw Jimmy reading a large newspaper.

"Well, young man!" he exclaimed. "They kept you late at school today."

"I actually went to the library after school to do my homework."

"Ah, so that's where you were!" Edith's voice wafted from the kitchen. "Did you ever think it might be a good idea to let us know when you'd be back?"

"Sorry, Edith," Seb replied. "I'm sort of used to doing my own thing."

"Huh!" she exclaimed. "The youth of today..." Her words were mercifully drowned out by the sizzle of another egg hitting the pan.

Seb took the opportunity to go to his room to change his clothes. He was amazed that this eccentric couple were friends of kind, gentle, diplomatic and tidy Mrs Thompson. Edith was certainly hard to please.

———

After a dinner of fried eggs, bacon and chips, Seb retreated to his room. He sat on the edge of the creaky bed, head in his hands. It was now 7:10pm. He had less than an hour before he had to be at Dad's. That was the last place he wanted to be right now, but if staying away meant putting Mum in danger, he was willing to sacrifice for her. And was there a possibility that his presence in the house would cause Dad to consider the matter of God, or would it be a reminder of his intense hatred for Christians? Dad had once told him that if he became a Christian, he would kill him. What if he decided to carry out his threat?

Maybe he should talk to Uncle Matt. He lifted the phone and

began to search through his contacts.

The doorbell rang and Seb paused. He could hear Jimmy shuffle to the door and pull it open. "We support our own choice of charities and we're not interested in giving anything to whatever cause it is you're representing." In spite of himself, Seb smiled. That was certainly a unique way to answer the door!

"I'm not collecting money, sir," came a familiar voice. Seb's smile died away.

"Oh, you're not? Well, that's something! We get a lot of beggars calling here. Then what is it?"

"My name is Alan Mitchelson, and I'm Seb's father."

"Seb? Who's Seb?"

Edith's voice joined in the conversation. "Jimmy, don't be so daft. That's that wee fella who's staying here."

"Oh, is *that* his name?" came Jimmy's amazed reply. "I thought it was something like Ted. I'm no good with names anyway."

"Don't worry, sir, I'm not much better," Dad's polite voice floated up the stairs.

"Are you here to visit him? Step inside." Edith took over the conversation.

"No, no, I just wanted to let him know that I'm expecting him later. He's coming back to live with me."

"He is? He didn't tell us that! Where do you live? And how come we're only hearing about you now? All we were told was that his mum wasn't well and he needed a place to stay for a wee while."

"I was away for a few days and I'm just back home. I was terribly annoyed when I heard the message on the answerphone about Julie and I'm sorry I wasn't home for Seb. But now that I'm back, he can live with me until his mum is feeling better. Thanks for looking after him."

"Oh, that was no problem!" simpered Edith. "He was a joy to have in the house."

Despite his growing dread, Seb nearly snorted with laughter. If that was true, she had a strange way of showing it.

The door closed and the old pair conferred in loud whispers.

"I wonder why the young man didn't tell us that he was moving back home."

"Ah, you know what teenagers are like. Moody and silent," declared Edith. "All the same, it's harder work than I thought. We're much too old for this kind of babysitting."

"Aw, Edith. He isn't that bad. You just don't like your routine being upset."

"Humph. Well, he's better being with family, don't you think?"

———

Seb gathered as many belongings as he could and lugged them downstairs.

"Will you be able to manage everything, young man?" asked Jimmy, hooking his thumbs into his braces.

"I think so," Seb replied. "There are two more bags upstairs, but I'll come back tomorrow for those."

"Very good," the old man replied. "I'd help you with them myself, but these knees aren't like they used to be. This old house is a-shaking and a-crumbling."

Old house? "Oh, you mean your body!"

"Hah! Maybe both," interjected Edith. "We need a lot of repairs done, but someone," she glared at her husband, "insists that he can do everything and we don't need a handyman." She crossed her arms and looked at Seb. "Well, what are you waiting for? We aren't prone to emotional farewells here, so you may head on your merry way."

Seb gathered his bags in his arms. "Thank you very much for everything."

Edith waved a hand at him.

"Look after yourself, young man," said Jimmy, dipping his head in farewell.

"Come on, you old goat, you'll see him tomorrow when he gets his stuff." Edith ushered her husband into the house and Seb set off down the street.

It didn't take him long to reach Dad's house. The bags weren't easy to carry; they kept slipping from his arms, but he'd have gladly walked all the way back to Mrs Thompson's instead.

He set the bags down on the doorstep. He was here, the place he thought he'd left behind for good. He couldn't understand why things had gone so badly wrong. How was this in God's plan?

He took a deep breath and opened the door.

Chapter Nineteen

As usual, the television was blaring. Dad was sprawled on the sofa, a blue beer can resting on his belly. He glanced around, a victorious grin spreading over his face, as Seb lugged his belongings through the door.

"You're here." He struggled to his feet, then pushed aside the clutter on the coffee table to set down his can. "Sensible."

Seb shrank from him as he came closer. The smell of cigarette smoke and alcohol transported him to the days when he and Mum lived here under the shadow of unpredictable anger and violence. "Am I in my old bedroom?" he asked, wanting to escape.

Dad laughed drily. "Where else would you be?"

Seb shrugged and made his way upstairs. He dumped the bags in the corner of the room, kicked the door closed and sank onto the bed. He felt defeated and alone. This was the last place on earth he'd wanted or expected to be.

———

Seb awoke during the night with the front door opening and closing. He lay in the dark and listened. Was Dad coming in or was he leaving? He leaned over the edge of the bed and lifted his phone to check the time. 2:15am. The house was silent. Dad must have gone out. Seb rubbed his eyes. Why was he only leaving now? He yawned and his eyelids closed. Time enough to figure it out in the morning…

———

"Hi! I'm Amanda." The tall, curvy redhead said, reaching out red-tipped fingers to Seb. He shook her hand, feeling as if he'd stepped into someone else's kitchen. Who was this woman and what was she doing here? Her hair lay in gentle curls against her shoulders and her lips matched her fingernails.

"I'm Seb," replied Seb. The look of confusion must have showed in his face, as Amanda laughed, a deep, throaty laugh.

"I know," she replied, reaching for the packet of cigarettes on the table and lighting one. She offered the packet to Seb.

"No, thanks. I don't smoke."

She waved a manicured hand. "You're Alan's son. He clearly didn't tell you about me."

Seb shook his head, then began to look in the cupboards.

"There's no food here. Your dad doesn't cook, you know."

"I know that," he said. "I was just looking for some breakfast."

Amanda pulled open the fridge and stepped back to let Seb see inside. Nothing but beer.

"What are you going to eat?" he asked her.

"I'll eat at work."

Footsteps sounded on the stairs and Dad appeared at the door, unshaven and dressed only in a pair of tracksuit bottoms.

"Well, you've met Amanda," he croaked, flinging an arm around her shoulders. "Isn't she something else?"

Seb looked at his shoes and scratched his head. How was he supposed to answer that question? He had no idea what she saw in Dad. He must be treating her better than he treated Mum. But what he really failed to understand was why Dad was so concerned with finding Mum when he had obviously moved on. And why had Seb been brought back into the middle of it?

He glanced at his watch and turned to leave the kitchen.

"Where are you going?" called Dad.

"Back upstairs," Seb answered.

"Don't let us chase you away. You live here!"

"I'm not running away. I have things to do."

"What sort of things? Homework?!" Dad asked sarcastically.

Seb shook his head and took a deep breath. "I'm going to read my Bible."

Dad's face changed in an instant. He lifted his arm from Amanda's shoulder and advanced towards Seb. "I thought you would have given all that up by now," he growled through gritted teeth. "Can't you see it's all a pack of lies? Matt certainly brainwashed you well this summer. It's a good job you're here now, so I can undo all the damage he did. How many times do I need to tell you that there is no God?"

Seb stood firm and breathed a silent prayer for wisdom and protection. "There *is* a God," he stated simply.

Dad took a step closer and raised a clenched fist. "Don't you *ever* say that to me again," he yelled. "I don't want to hear that name mentioned in this house. You hear me?"

Seb nodded.

Dad grabbed him by the arm and shook. "You hear me?" he repeated.

"Come on, Alan, I think he understands," Amanda said soothingly. She smiled apologetically at Seb.

Dad let go of Seb's arm and he fled up the stairs. He could still feel Dad's fingers biting into his arm and he was certain it was going to bruise. Not for the first time, he was astounded at the rage and venom he saw in Dad's face when God and the Bible were mentioned. Seb couldn't understand why he was so vicious and so full of hatred.

———

Seb placed the correct change on the counter. It was a meagre breakfast, but he needed to keep enough money for his lunch. Lifting the cereal bar and bottle of orange juice, he left the shop. He grimaced. Much as he hated the idea, he was going to have to ask Dad for money. After today, there would be none left. He wondered if he would blackmail him and make him promise that he wouldn't read his Bible. *Well, in that case,* thought Seb, *I'll just have to go hungry.*

He tore the wrapper from the bar and took a bite. Before long, it was gone. It hardly took the edge off his hunger and he tried to ignore the empty feeling in his stomach.

As he approached the school gates, he could see a boy getting out of a silver car. Edward. Seb hurried to catch up. He felt he needed to explain his less-than-friendly behaviour yesterday.

"Hi, Seb," Edward greeted him as Seb rushed towards him. "How are you today?"

"I'm well. How are you?"

"Ah, Seb!" he laughed. "I've never been better. Come and I'll tell you why." Edward led the way into the school. As they walked down the corridor towards the classroom, Seb glanced at Edward. He was beaming and he looked as if he was bursting to tell Seb something. Maybe they were returning to Malaysia? Seb felt sad at the prospect. He'd enjoyed having Edward as a friend.

The form classroom was empty. No one else had arrived so early.

"I have been reading the Bible you gave me," Edward began.

"That's good," Seb said. "Can you understand it?"

"Not everything," Edward said, laughing. "But I have found it a fascinating book. I understand that there is one true God, the One who made the earth and the animals and human beings. I'm sure the Bible is God's Word."

"What makes you so sure?" asked Seb, curious. They had discussed various topics over the past few weeks, but had only touched briefly on this one.

"I researched on the internet," replied Edward. "There are many reasons – prophecy fulfilled, the accuracy of the historical details, particularly Luke's writings, the way that it has been preserved so accurately... you know about the Dead Sea scrolls, right?"

Seb nodded. Uncle Matt had told him this story. The Dead Sea scrolls were found by Bedouin shepherd boys in a cave in Qumran in 1946. They didn't know what they were, but finally the scrolls made their way into the hands of experts who determined they were an ancient copy of the book of Isaiah. Comparing them with the current copies of Isaiah showed very little variation over thousands of years, proving that God is able to preserve His Word.

"So, if the Bible is God's Word," continued Edward, "then there really are only two places after death: heaven and hell. And I know I'm a sinner, and sinners can't be in heaven without their sins forgiven."

Seb nodded. "But Christ died for sinners."

"Yes!" exclaimed Edward. "He died for *me*! I trusted Him and now I'm a Christian. Like you, Seb!"

Seb's smile widened to a grin. How amazing to know that Edward was saved and on his way to heaven. The events of that morning receded, now replaced with joy. "That's fantastic news, Edward!"

"What's fantastic news?" a voice interjected.

The boys turned round. Madison and Zoe were standing behind them, each holding a lever arch file.

"I was telling Seb that I'm now a Christian," said Edward, smiling.

Madison frowned at Seb. "Seb!" she exclaimed. "I can't believe you!"

Seb looked at Madison in shock. What was she accusing him of doing?

"You shouldn't interfere with people's religion. That's their own business. Who cares whether someone is a Hindu or a Buddhist or a Muslim or a Jew or a Christian or a...a..." She broke off, unable to name any more religions.

"Madison, there is only one God, and only one way to God," Edward told her. "I was brought up a Buddhist and I can see clearly that Jesus Christ is the only way."

Madison looked at Seb indignantly. "You have him brainwashed!" she exclaimed.

Seb shook his head. "No. Edward thought this through for himself," he told her.

"Well, what do your parents think?" she asked Edward with a slight smile.

Edward's head dropped and he poked the chair leg with his toe. "I-I haven't told them yet," he stammered.

"Why not?" persisted Madison.

Edward lifted his head and looked at Seb, sadness in his brown eyes. "They won't be very happy," he replied.

Madison turned to look at Seb. "There you go. You aren't content with your own family being on the rocks, you're trying to break up his family as well." With that, she marched off to her seat. Zoe followed, but glanced around at the boys. Funny, she almost looked sorry for Edward.

"Is that true, that your parents won't be happy?" asked Seb, when the girls were out of earshot.

Edward nodded.

"Why? Is it because you have abandoned their religion?"

"Partly," Edward said. "They will think that I'm giving up my Malaysian Chinese culture and becoming Western. Another reason they will be unhappy is because that I won't be partaking in their Buddhist practices. And that means that, when they die, I won't be burning hell money for them. They will worry that their spirits will wander alone and hungry in the unseen world. It's a big thing for Buddhists to abandon their religion. I had a distant cousin who decided that he didn't want anything to do with religion. It nearly sent his parents crazy."

And Seb thought that he had problems! "We'll have to pray for your parents," he said. "My dad, too. This morning he told me that he never again wanted to hear me say that there is a God. He was getting really angry."

"Did he threaten to hit you?" asked Edward, eyes wide.

"Not directly, but I think that's what he meant."

"I didn't know you were living with your dad."

Seb smiled wryly. "I wasn't, until last night." He proceeded to tell him the story until Mr Symons arrived to mark the roll.

"You're welcome to come home with me anytime," Edward told Seb on the way to physics class.

"Thank you, but maybe I'd better stay away until you've told your parents the news."

Edward nodded. He looked troubled.

"God won't let you down," Seb told him. "His Word is full of promises. One of my favourites is 'I will never leave you nor forsake you.' "

They entered the room. "I like that," Edward said, smiling. "Thank you, Seb. I'm glad I came to Belfast."

Chapter Twenty

"Well done, Seb," Mrs Jones twittered as she set the marked maths test on the desk in front of him. "Your hard work has paid off." She smiled and moved on to the next desk, catching her foot on the leg of Seb's chair on the way past. The class roared with laughter as the stack of maths tests floated through the air, before coming to rest like autumn leaves on the floor.

Seb leaned over and gathered as many as he could reach, then gave them to the teacher. As she continued around the room, Seb looked at his paper. A 'B'! He smiled. That was better than he was expecting. Edward glanced around and Seb gave him a thumbs up sign. He certainly couldn't have done it without Edward's tuition.

It had been a few weeks since Edward had got saved. As he had predicted, his parents were anything but happy. They were still courteous and polite to Seb on the few occasions that he visited the house, but made their disappointment and displeasure known to Edward regularly.

Edward, however, hadn't let their attitude dampen his enthusiasm for his newfound faith in Christ, and had even gone with Seb to the little church he had found a few streets from Dad's house.

Even now, Seb was amazed that the place had been there all those years when he had lived in the area and he hadn't even known. He couldn't blame the people who attended that church; if anyone from the church had ever called with Christian literature, they would have been sent swiftly on their way.

Mrs Jones returned to the front of the classroom. "Okay, class," she called, grabbing a pen and gesturing wildly with it. "Let's go through the questions on your test. It's important that you know how to do these. They are very common examination questions…"

Despite Seb's best efforts, he struggled to concentrate. Instead, he couldn't help but think of the last piece of work that a teacher had marked and handed back. Seb knew he was taking a big risk writing what he did, but he couldn't lie. So it was no surprise when the essay was flung onto his desk, covered in red pen, and a '20%' on the front. Seb had been strangely cheered that Mr Symons hadn't given him zero. An essay on 'the process of evolution', where Seb had written extensively about how DNA couldn't possibly have evolved, wasn't something that was going to make Mr Symons very happy. Seb had hidden a smile when he turned to the back and read the teacher's comment. *While you have obviously researched and thought about your chosen topic, you will gain no marks in an examination if you do not answer the given question as taught in accordance with the syllabus.*

Since then, Mr Symons had largely ignored Seb in class. Seb didn't think, for one minute, that his basic essay had convinced the teacher of the existence of God. But maybe, just maybe, he had gone a little way in showing Mr Symons that far cleverer Christians than Seb had thought these things through and weren't ignoring facts and scientific evidence.

"And now for question eight." Mrs Jones' voice broke into his thoughts. Seb blinked and lifted his pen. This was one he hadn't got right. He hoped it would make sense when Mrs Jones explained it.

At the end of the class, Mrs Jones trotted down to Seb's desk. "I must congratulate you again on your wonderful test," she said. "Did you know you almost got an 'A'?"

Seb shook his head.

"If you work as hard as you have been," she continued, her eyelashes fluttering up and down, "you will get an 'A' in the exams at the end of term."

"Really?" He'd never had an 'A' in anything in his life.

"Seb," went on Mrs Jones, "why the sudden change? Last year you never did your homework, you never listened in class, schoolwork was the last thing on your mind. What has happened?"

Seb smiled. An opportunity to explain the 'reason for the hope' in him, as the verse said. "Over the summer, I became a Christian," he told her.

She frowned doubtfully at him. "But we are all Christians," she said. "We live in a Christian country. Some are more religious than others, I admit."

Seb shook his head. "A Christian is someone who repents of their sin, and trusts in the Lord Jesus Christ for salvation. He died for us, and rose again."

"Oh, yes, that's Easter," replied Mrs Jones. "But I'm a good person; I don't have to repent."

"Everyone has sinned, Mrs Jones," replied Seb. "The Bible says so."

The little lady frowned. "Maybe other people, Seb. But not me. We get into heaven when God sees that the good deeds that we have done outweigh our bad ones. I'm a good person." She nodded to confirm her own statement.

Seb sighed. He felt so sorry for this lady. She thought she was going to heaven, and instead, she was going to hell, and didn't even realise it.

"Mrs Jones, I must tell you, God says our righteousnesses are like filthy rags. He loves you, but He is holy and perfect. God can't bring sinners into heaven unless they have believed in the Lord Jesus Christ and been cleansed from their sin."

Mrs Jones gave a tight little smile, and tapped the desk once with a petite hand. "Keep up the good work," she said, then turned and walked back to the front of the room.

"What was Mrs Jones saying to you?" asked Edward, as they walked towards the canteen.

Seb recounted his conversation. "I feel so sorry for her. She thinks her religion and good works are going to get her into heaven."

Edward nodded. "You told her the truth, Seb. Maybe she'll search the Bible for herself and one day trust Christ."

———

The house was quiet when Seb returned home later that afternoon. His homework hadn't taken long today. He went straight upstairs to his bedroom and changed his clothes. There was no point in looking for a snack in the kitchen. Instead, he'd bought a supply of cereal bars, crisps and juice, with money Dad had given him. He had just pulled out a bottle of fizzy orange and a peanut cereal bar from his stash under the bed when his phone rang. Uncle Matt.

"Well, Seb, how are you getting on?"

"Yes, fine," he replied. Uncle Matt had phoned twice since he'd returned from his weekend at Cherryhill, but he still couldn't bring himself to tell him what had happened or that he was living with Dad again.

"School going okay?"

"Yes," Seb replied. This was safe ground. He'd already told him that Edward had got saved, so he talked about him, his biology essay, his maths test, and the discussion with Mrs Jones earlier.

Uncle Matt listened, only speaking to say *uh-huh* every so often.

"And what about the cows?" asked Seb. "Any more calves this week?"

"Two new ones this week," replied Uncle Matt. "Both bulls, but the cows are doing well." He continued to talk about the farm, then – "Is your mum there, Seb?"

Seb gulped. "No, she's not," he answered.

"At work?"

"I'm not actually sure where she is." Technically, it wasn't a lie.

"Karen has been trying to phone her, but she hasn't been answering her phone. We were just wondering if everything is all right."

"Yes, it's fine," replied Seb. He hated deceiving his uncle, but he was terrified that if Uncle Matt knew where he was, he would insist on Seb coming to stay at Cherryhill at once. And when Dad found out Seb was gone, well, he didn't dare think what would happen to Mum.

There was a pause. "Well, as long as everything is okay. Good to talk to you, Seb. We'll have to have you back here for another weekend soon."

"That'd be nice," Seb told him, "but I have a lot of homework these days."

"We'll keep it in mind."

They ended the call and Seb threw the phone onto the bed, breathing a sigh of relief. He didn't think Uncle Matt suspected anything, but he would need to tell Mum to at least send Karen a text message to relieve her suspicions.

His mind drifted to Mum. He'd kept in touch, but hadn't seen her since the day she left for the safe accommodation. She'd told Seb that he was allowed to visit, but he felt it would be better if he didn't know where she was. He hadn't told her either that he was living with Dad. She'd enough to worry about.

Seb lifted the cereal bar and the juice. He was fed up always staying in his bedroom. Maybe he could sit in the living room when the house was empty.

Carrying his snack downstairs, he pushed open the living room door. As usual, the coffee table was piled high with newspapers and magazines. An ashtray crowned the mountain, and a pile of beer cans rested in the corner of the room. Obviously Amanda wasn't going to clean Dad's house for him when she was here.

Seb wrinkled his nose at the stale smell, before flinging open a window. It might be quite breezy outside, but the room needed fresh air. He lifted another pile of odds and ends – phone charger, dirty tea-stained mug, a screwdriver – off the armchair and sat down to eat his snack.

As he ate, he looked around the room. Clutter and rubbish everywhere. He wondered if he should clean up a bit, or, if he did it once, would he always end up with the job? Shoving the last of the cereal bar into his mouth, he stood up. Dad likely wouldn't even notice anyway. All the same, getting rid of those beer cans might help the smell of the room.

It took Seb a long time to find the bin liners. He finally located the roll squeezed into a too-full drawer of cling film, sandwich bags and tin foil. Seb wasn't sure when the last time any of those items had been used. Mum had never really cooked when they all lived here, instead buying microwave meals and carry outs. He pulled a bag off the roll and rubbed the end together until it began to open, then gave it two good shakes. In the living room, he cleared the pile in the corner, then tipped the contents of the ashtray into the bag.

Seb set the bin liner on the floor beside the table and began to sort through the newspapers and magazines. He shook the TV remote out from the middle of the sports section of the paper on the top of the pile, and set it aside.

Buried in the pile, he found two mugs, a set of keys, another phone charger and an unopened padded envelope. Setting the items aside, he continued to work on clearing the mess.

When he finally could see the top of the coffee table, he tied a knot in the top of the bin bag and took it outside to throw it into the grey wheelie bin.

After washing his hands, he made his way back to the living room. Pausing in the doorway, he stopped to admire the difference his clean-up efforts had made. The room could do with a good dusting and vacuuming, but Seb had no idea where either a duster or even the vacuum cleaner might be. Come to think of it, Mum likely took it with her. Dad wouldn't have missed it.

He plopped onto the sofa and lifted the envelope he'd set aside earlier. What on earth could it be? It was unaddressed and felt heavy. He pressed his fingers around the edges. It didn't appear to have corners, so it wasn't a book, but whatever was inside seemed to fill all the available space.

Seb turned it over. It was stuck shut. He tugged the edge of the flap and it began to let go. Gently pulling along the seal, he managed to prise it open. He turned it upside down and shook it. A clear plastic-wrapped package fell with a thud onto his knee. His eyes widened in disbelief and shock.

The package was full of white, granular powder.

Chapter Twenty-One

Seb didn't have to look twice to know that what was contained in the package was an illegal substance. He figured by the look of it that it was likely cocaine, classified as a Class A drug. He'd seen it in much smaller quantities around school in the past. He knew that Dad had been acting shiftily over the past few months, but he had ignored the growing suspicion that he was involved in illegal activities. It all made sense, though – the increase in available money, the strange phone calls, and coming and going at odd hours.

Seb groaned. Things were swiftly going downhill. It was bad enough that Dad was a drunk, a wife-beater and an adulterer, but now he was working in the drugs trade. He turned the package over in his hands. He wasn't sure exactly how much this was worth, but he had a fair idea it was pretty valuable. His first thought was to get rid of it, maybe flush it down the toilet, but he knew that if he did that, he wouldn't live to see another day.

Sliding the package inside the envelope, he pressed the flap back down to reseal it. He held it out at arm's length. Not bad. No one would have ever known it had been opened. He set it on the coffee table and winced. Those newspapers had clearly been serving a purpose. There was nothing for it but to bring them all back in again.

He had just finished reconstructing the mountain from memory, envelope in the middle of the pile and ashtray on the top, when Dad walked in. Seb forced his face to stay expressionless and looked round at Dad. He glared at Seb.

"What do you think you're doing?" he said.

Seb took a deep breath. "Cleaning up," he replied. "Look at this mess." He waved a hand at the coffee table.

"Well, it's my mess and I don't want you interfering with it. Stop being such a sissy, cleaning and tidying. Next thing you'll be wearing a frilly apron and baking scones. Go on; get out!"

Seb shrugged. "The room stinks," he told him, lifting the bag of cans. As he stood up, he spotted one of the mugs he'd forgotten to build into the pile. He lifted it as unobtrusively as possible and carried it through to the kitchen to dump in the sink with the twenty other dirty mugs which resided there.

As he came back inside after throwing the bin bag away for the second time that afternoon, he heard the noise of the TV. He took a quick glance into the living room before he climbed the stairs. Dad was sprawled on the sofa, can of beer in one hand, cigarette in the other.

Seb sat down on the bed and reached out his foot to kick the door shut. Dad seemed relaxed and Seb was relieved that he hadn't noticed anything amiss. He wondered what Dad's role was. Surely he wasn't a dealer, pushing drugs onto poor, addicted young people, helping to destroy their lives and their futures. Did he use violence to extract money from them? A sudden thought struck Seb – was it possible that Dad used drugs himself? He knew that some drugs affected people's minds so much that it caused them to become unreasonably violent. It might help to explain why he almost killed Mum.

The noise from the TV abruptly stopped and, in the sudden silence, Dad's voice rang out loud and clear.

"Yes, Billy. Going good. Yourself?" Seb frowned. Who was Billy? He knew quite a few of Dad's friends, but that was a name he didn't recognise. He dropped to the floor and pressed his ear to it. If Dad dropped his voice, he still wanted to be able to hear every word.

"Yes, I have it... No problem... Is that the petrol station on the left or the right? There's one on each side of the road...Beside the big church?...Of course! What do you take me for?" Dad sounded indignant. "I'm not stupid!" He lapsed into silence, then, "Sorry. I know that." Seb blinked. Dad sounded chastened. He wondered what the other person had just said to cause Dad to actually apologise. And who was this Billy person, who had such a control over him?

Seb silently got up from the floor and flopped onto the bed, replaying in his mind the conversation that had just taken place. He was in no doubt that it related to the package resting amongst the newspapers downstairs. He figured that Dad was going to have to take it to a petrol station at some stage, probably tonight. But which petrol station?

Pulling out his phone, he typed 'large church Belfast' into the search engine and began to scroll through the lengthy list. How would he ever find the church they were talking about? Come to think of it, he didn't know if the meeting place was even in Belfast at all. He couldn't help but shake his head at the audacity of transferring a package of drugs right beside a church.

Seb's stomach rumbled and he glanced at his watch. 5:33pm. He wondered if Dad had any thought of dinner at all. There was no point in waiting – if he didn't go and find something to eat, he would go hungry. He pulled open his bedroom door and went downstairs. The TV was on again. Seb poked his head into the room. Dad was draining the last few drops of the beer.

"What about dinner?" asked Seb.

Dad's head turned to look at Seb. "What about it?" he asked rudely.

Seb bit his lip. "I'm getting hungry. I might go for chips. Do you want some?"

Dad looked at his watch. "I'm heading out shortly. I'll get something when I'm out."

Seb nodded. "Okay." He hesitated, scuffing his toe against the doorframe. "Um, Dad...?"

"What is it now?"

"I... I'm running out of money again..."

Dad laughed. "Ha! More money? So your mum hasn't any to spare you. She certainly didn't save as much money by leaving me as she hoped, did she?"

"That was hardly the reason why she left!" Seb exclaimed indignantly.

"Really?" Dad chuckled. "Well, whatever it was, her little plan backfired."

Seb narrowed his eyes and clenched his jaw. Dad could be so obnoxious.

Dad chucked the beer can into the empty corner and struggled to his feet. He stretched. His blue t-shirt rose, revealing his fat, hairy beer belly, then he reached for his jacket which had been flung over the back of the sofa.

"Here you go." He handed a couple of notes to Seb. "Don't spend it all at once." He sniggered.

Seb glanced at the notes. It would buy him a couple of meals, if he was careful. "I thought you had loads of money now." The words were out of him before he knew it.

Dad turned and stared at Seb. Seb straightened his back and tried to stare back without flinching. The raucous cheers of celebration over a goal scored in a football field miles from Belfast filled the room. Dad broke eye contact. "Of course I do," he blustered. "But do you think I'd leave it lying around the house? Ever heard of banks?" he asked sarcastically, pulling on his jacket and fishing his car keys from the pocket.

Seb pocketed the money and went upstairs for his sweatshirt. By the time he came down, his dad had left. He peered between the curtains. Dad's car was turning left at the end of the street. Seb checked the newspaper pile. The envelope was gone. Sinking onto the sofa his dad had vacated minutes earlier, he closed his eyes and tried to envisage a large church with two petrol stations nearby. It could be anywhere. His stomach rumbled again and he stood up. A gravy chip sounded pretty good right now.

———

The chip shop was full of people – men, women, teenagers and even some children standing with their backs pressed against the large front window. Two women sat on the small faux leather seat, babies on their knees. The air was heavy with the scent of deep-fried food, and the shouts of order numbers accompanied by "two cheeseburgers and a sausage supper" competed with the hum of the extractor fans.

Seb pushed his way through the crowd. An overweight woman was giving a lengthy order to the bored-looking youth manning the till.

"Fifty-eight," a deep, husky voice called, and one of the women on the seat stood up, adjusting her baby on her hip, to collect her order. As she left, another customer pushed into the small shop.

"Hi, Seb." A tap on the shoulder accompanied the words and he turned round.

"Oh, hi, Zoe," he replied. "This place is so busy tonight."

She nodded. "And I'm starving!" she exclaimed.

"Me too," grinned Seb.

Zoe pointed behind Seb. He turned round. The lady had finally finished her order and had moved off.

"Sorry," he told the cashier.

The youth shrugged and rolled his eyes. "What are you having?" he drawled.

"Gravy chip. And a bottle of coke." He handed over his cash. Receipt and change in hand, he glanced around the crowded shop. He found a small space along the wall and squeezed between two other customers. His stomach growled. He hoped his order of chips smothered in gravy wouldn't take too long.

Zoe joined him when she'd placed her order.

"So, what's up?" she asked.

"Not much."

As they chatted about school and homework, Seb's mind drifted back to the package that Dad would likely be delivering right about now.

"Um, Zoe," Seb began. "Do you know where..." He paused. Zoe might wonder why he was asking.

She looked at him quizzically.

He decided to go for it. "Do you know of any big churches near two filling stations?"

Zoe laughed. "That's kind of vague, Seb. Do you have any other details? Do you know what the church looks like, or what area it's in?"

Seb shook his head. "It doesn't matter. How did you get on in the geography test?"

She scrunched up her nose. "Mm. Not so good! What about you?"

"Better than I'd hoped," he replied. "But Edward got 100%."

"Seriously?! He is so unbelievably clever, like. What's he even doing at our school?"

"Seventy-two! Gravy chip!"

Seb glanced at his receipt. "That's me." He walked to the desk and, after salt and vinegar were applied, collected his paper-wrapped package. He waved at Zoe. "See you tomorrow."

As he stepped out the door, he heard Zoe calling. "Wait, Seb!"

He turned back. The lady was shaking a generous amount of salt and vinegar over Zoe's chips, then wrapping them with a skilful hand. Zoe grabbed the package and ran after Seb.

"I've remembered!"

Seb frowned.

"The church! I think I know where it is. It's a huge church and there's a petrol station right beside it and another one right across the street."

Seb nodded excitedly. "That sounds right!" he said. "How far away is it?"

"Fifteen minutes' walk," Zoe replied. "What time is the service?"

"Service?"

"Aren't you wanting to go to one of the services?"

"Oh!" Seb shrugged. "I'm not sure. I just want to have a look." He hoped that wasn't a lie.

"Okay," replied Zoe, using her plastic fork to point to the right. "It's this way. Let's go."

"It's fine," said Seb. "If you give me the directions, I'm sure I can find my own way."

"It's no bother. I'm not doing anything tonight anyway." Her made-up eyes looked sad for an instant. What was Zoe's story anyway? Seb had never thought to ask.

They set off along the road, eating as they walked. Dad would likely be gone by the time they arrived, but, just in case, he hoped that Zoe would leave before they got there. The last thing Seb wanted was for Zoe to witness the transaction too.

Chapter Twenty-Two

Seb scratched his head. What *were* all these services? Truth Trotters? Plugged In? Worship Extravaganza? Wild 'n' Free? Breakfast Breeze-Through? Jesus-Loves-Me-And-So-Should-I Self-Esteem Group?

He turned to Zoe, confused. "Do you know what these are?" He gestured at the notice board just inside the main door.

Zoe shook her head. "I haven't a clue, but here's someone who might be able to help you."

A lady with short, burgundy hair and a tight mini-dress minced across on skyscraper heels, a bright red smile pasted on her perfect face. "Hi, I'm Wanda. I'm the receptionist. Can I help you young people?"

"We were looking at the list of services–"

"Oh, I'm dreadfully sorry," Wanda interrupted. "The Jericho Nightclub is only on a Saturday night."

"Jericho Nightclub?" repeated Zoe.

"Yes. Are you familiar with the story of how Joshua and the army marched around the city of Jericho and the walls came down?"

Seb nodded. "But what has that got to do with a *nightclub*?"

Wanda gave a loud guffaw. It reverberated around the tiled floor and painted walls of the lobby. Who was this lady? Was she actually a member or did she just work for this church? "You remember the trumpets which they blew?"

Seb nodded uncertainly.

"There you go. Play the music loud enough and the walls will fall down and this church will march forward! Conquering through music and dance!" She pumped a small, manicured fist in the air.

Seb frowned. Her logic was terribly flawed. It wasn't the music which made the walls come down. It was God's power. "Do you have a prayer meeting? Or a Bible study?"

"Oh, yes!" laughed Wanda. "Plugged In is when we connect with God. And Breakfast Breeze-Through is our biggest weekly study on offer. We enjoy a good breakfast, an inspirational talk and then spend a few minutes on Bible study. We aim to cover the Bible in a year."

Seb frowned. He figured that the group was aptly named. "Well, what about the gospel? Don't you tell people they are sinners? That the Lord Jesus Christ shed His blood to save them?"

Wanda recoiled. "Oh, we don't use words like that! People don't want to hear that. It's so wonderful to focus on how much we mean to God."

"That might be so," replied Seb. "But you need to tell people that if they never trust Christ, they are going to be in hell for all eternity."

The smile disappeared from Wanda's face and she turned back

to her desk. "It was good to meet you, but perhaps you should look for another church." She gave them a nod and tight smile. "Good evening."

Seb breathed a sigh of relief as they left the building. He wondered if everyone who attended was like Wanda, or if she was the exception to the rule. Could God really be in a place like that? They seemed to be more interested in worshipping self than God.

Seb scanned the carpark of the filling station from the high steps of the church. There had been no sign of Dad when they arrived. Seb wasn't surprised. By the time he had walked to the chip shop, got his chips and walked here, Dad would have been here and gone ages ago.

"So I take it you aren't going to attend that church?" asked Zoe.

Seb turned to look at her. She had a bemused look on her face.

"Definitely not!" he exclaimed. "Do you think they read the Bible? Wanda doesn't seem to, or if she does, she only reads part of it."

"Well, they do have a Breeze-Through!" giggled Zoe as she walked down the steps to the bricked pavement which stretched from the church to the road.

Seb grunted. "It sounds as if they're more interested in the breakfast than in the Bible. What did she say? A few minutes a week? To cover the Bible in a year? They wouldn't even have time to read it, never mind study it! And a self-esteem class?" Seb was on a roll. "Do you know what the Bible says about us? 'We are all like an unclean thing' and 'all have sinned and fall short of the glory of God.' That woman is trying to say that we are all wonderful and important! Is she crazy? I mean, the Bible does say we are fearfully and wonderfully made, but it's very clear we are sinners–"

"Seb! *Seb!*" Zoe interrupted. "Calm down! You're getting all wound up."

Zoe was right. He took a deep breath. "I just get annoyed when I see people using God's name to make up a false religion. They're deceiving people into thinking they are going to heaven when they're not. It's true that God loves us, but He hates our sin and we can't be in heaven without having our sins forgiven."

"I know," replied Zoe, as she pushed open the gate and walked through onto the pavement.

Seb followed, and closed the gate behind him. "You do?" he asked, as Zoe's words filtered through his righteous indignation.

She nodded her head. "I used to go to Sunday school at the wee church around the corner... Seb, is that your dad?"

Seb froze. "Where?"

"Over there, right against the wall of the shop."

Zoe was right. It was Dad. Seb didn't know where his car was, but he would recognise him anywhere. He was leaning against the wall with a cigarette in his hand, watching a tall, blonde lady fill her sports car with petrol. Seb didn't think he'd seen them yet.

"This way," he hissed to Zoe, as he quickly turned around and headed back towards the church. She stopped and frowned at him, then followed.

"Why don't you want him to see you?" she asked.

Seb ignored her question. He opened the gate to the church again and slipped through. Zoe followed, too confused to do anything else. He stepped off the path and walked across the neatly manicured lawns to the perimeter. Here, a green laurel hedge hid the chain link fence and enclosed the church grounds from the real world in a band of bright green.

Seb squatted down and looked under the hedge. The leaves and branches weren't so plentiful at the bottom, and he could see the garage forecourt plainly. He sat down and Zoe sank down beside him. "Ugh, the grass is all wet!" she exclaimed, raising herself up to an awkward crouching position.

"Shh!" Seb hissed. He could see Dad. He was still leaning against the wall, smoking his cigarette. The blonde had finished at the petrol pump and was walking back to her car from the shop.

As the red sports car left the forecourt, another car pulled in. An athletically-built man sprang out and began to fill his car.

"Hey!" exclaimed Zoe. "That's my Uncle Nigel!"

"Be quiet!" whispered Seb. "He'll wonder what we're doing, hiding under a hedge at a church."

"Well, what *are* we doing, hiding under a hedge at a church?" asked Zoe.

"I'll tell you later," promised Seb. He hoped she would forget about it. Zoe was about the last person he'd have chosen to be with him when he witnessed his dad passing along a suspicious package. She and Madison were well known for gossiping to each other.

They watched as Nigel filled his car and went to the shop to pay. Dad finished his cigarette, dropped the butt and ground it out with his heel, then pulled out another and lit it.

"Should he be smoking at a petrol station?" whispered Zoe.

"Probably not," replied Seb. "But Dad doesn't worry about details like that."

Nigel exited the shop, a white carrier bag in his hand. But instead of heading for his car, he turned left and walked past the racks of plants at the front of the shop, then turned the corner. Seb gasped as he walked up to Dad, and leaned against the wall beside him. Was Zoe's uncle really Dad's contact?

The two men appeared to exchange words, then Dad removed a brown padded envelope from inside his coat and handed it to Nigel. Nigel quickly dropped it into his carrier bag and walked back to his car. Dad continued smoking his cigarette as if he had all the time in the world.

Zoe turned to Seb, eyes wide. "I didn't know Uncle Nigel knew your dad!"

"Neither did I," he replied.

She blinked as she watched Nigel's black BMW leave the

forecourt. "I'll have to ask him how he knows your dad."

"No, Zoe! Don't say anything." He glanced back at Dad. Dad had pushed off from the wall and was walking towards the road. Seb figured his car wasn't too far away; Dad didn't like to walk any distance. He watched as Dad turned right and crossed the street to the other filling station. Seb stood up and peered over the hedge. He could just about see the form of Dad getting into his car, which was parked in one of the spaces at the side of the forecourt. Seb wondered how long he'd been here – was it possible he'd have been waiting in his car at the other petrol station as they walked past? He desperately hoped not.

Seb sat back down as Dad drove out of the petrol station. Whether he'd seen them or not, Seb didn't want to take any risks. When he was sure that Dad would be far enough away, he made his way back to the gate. Zoe followed. "Seb, what do you think was in the package?"

"Maybe something to do with work," he said, shrugging.

They stepped onto the pavement for the second time that evening. "I'm not really sure what Uncle Nigel works at," she said. "I mean, he always has nice cars and good phones, but he's usually at home during the day." She looked away, biting her lip. "I think he works from home. He's always on the internet..."

Seb looked at Zoe incredulously. Was she trying to cover up for her uncle, or did she genuinely not know?

"What?" she asked as Seb continued to frown at her. "Why are you staring at me like that?"

"Do you really not know what that was all about?" He waved his hand in the direction of the petrol station.

"Do you?" Zoe sidestepped his question.

Seb waggled his head in a combination of a nod and a shake. "I don't know for sure, but I have my suspicions," he replied.

Zoe narrowed her eyes at Seb. "What kind of suspicions? Do you think Uncle Nigel is actually up to something illegal?"

Seb was confused. Surely Zoe knew what they had just witnessed. She wasn't stupid. Drugs were a common sight at school and lots of the kids he knew had some link with criminal organisations. Drug dealing was a big part of those organisations' activities.

"You think that package contained drugs, don't you?" she said. She didn't seem to need an answer. "I can't believe you're accusing Uncle Nigel of being a drug dealer!"

Seb stared at Zoe. "Well, what do you think was in that package?" he asked.

"I haven't a clue," she said brightly as she threw her hands in the air in a couldn't-care-less gesture. "I'll ask him later if you want."

Seb gulped. "Please Zoe, don't do that," he pleaded.

"Why not?" She narrowed her eyes at Seb. "You're going to report him, aren't you?"

Seb shrugged. He hadn't thought what he would do after he

witnessed the handover. And yet...

"You are, aren't you? How dare you tell on Uncle Nigel? He's always so nice to me and buys me really good presents for my birthday and Christmas. And he's my mum's favourite brother; she pretty much brought him up. It would kill her! I can't stand you, Seb Mitchelson." She threw a look of disgust at him and marched off.

Seb rubbed a hand over his face. By now, he was really sorry that Zoe had watched the handover. In fact, he was beginning to wish that he hadn't seen it either. He wished that he could erase it from his memory and forget every detail. But he couldn't.

What was he going to do now?

Chapter Twenty-Three

Dad's car wasn't parked at the kerb outside the house. Seb glanced around. It wasn't anywhere on the street either. He had likely gone straight to the pub after he left the filling station. Someday he was either going to have an accident or get caught by the police. Seb hoped it would be the latter. Dad seemed to think that laws were optional and Seb wondered if the car was even taxed or insured. Come to think of it – had Dad even passed a driving test?

Seb turned his key in the door and went inside. The house was quiet, just the way he'd left it earlier. He closed and locked the door and went into the kitchen for a drink of water. Those chips had left him feeling very thirsty.

He washed a glass that he found on the bench beside the sink and filled it with water. He drained it in one go and refilled it, then carried it upstairs to his room. He kicked off his shoes and flopped onto his bed. The scene at the filling station played itself over in his mind. Dad, with a package of drugs, handing them over to his contact, who was Zoe's uncle. He should probably phone the police.

But what would he tell them? They might believe him, but they'd hardly come and arrest Dad on Seb's word alone. There was no point in asking Zoe, she seemed to be so fond of her uncle that she would deny she saw anything. And, anyway, they would need evidence. Maybe someone else saw the exchange? Or surely there were CCTV cameras around, there always were at filling stations in case people drove off without paying. But would Dad be so stupid as to pass on a package of drugs in full view of CCTV cameras? Seb knew Dad wasn't the most intelligent man on the planet, but surely he wasn't that daft. All the same, perhaps he should take a wee detour tomorrow just to make sure. Then he'd maybe phone the police.

———

Instead of going straight to the library as he usually did after school, Seb walked back to the filling station. It wasn't very far and he was glad of the walk to clear his head. He'd found it difficult to concentrate in class and more than once he caught himself trying to listen in on Zoe's and Madison's whispered conversation. He desperately hoped that, for once, Zoe wasn't telling her best friend absolutely everything that happened in her life. She had done a good job of ignoring Seb that day anyway.

Madison was much more outspoken than Zoe; Zoe just seemed to follow along with whatever Madison suggested most of the time. Seb thought back to their conversation about the church last night. He'd been surprised to hear she knew all about the gospel. He hadn't known she'd attended Sunday school, but then, how would he have known? Until this summer, he hadn't had the slightest interest in anything to do with religion. He would have been the last person she would have wanted to tell. He wondered what her current thoughts were on the subject. Had she rejected the whole message or would she be willing to go back to church some night?

He could see the filling station ahead. It looked just as busy as it had been last night. Seb was amazed at the way that Dad could pass on a package so brazenly and in front of so many people. Maybe the location was chosen for its busyness – the more people around, the less suspicion they might arouse.

Seb walked across the forecourt. He could see CCTV cameras above the pumps, pointing to each side. Where Dad was standing, he would have been hidden from these. He spotted another one at the outside corner of the shop, but again, this was pointing away from the side wall.

Seb went into the shop and chose a chocolate bar and a bottle of apple juice. After paying, he exited the shop and took the route Nigel had taken, past the plants and around the corner of the building. He stopped to open his juice in the spot where the transaction had taken place. He could see the church on the hill and the hedge where he and Zoe had hidden last night. The car wash was farther to his left, against the fence, and an air compressor was near the exit. He glanced to his left. The only CCTV camera that he could see seemed to be pointing towards the car wash. Dad had picked his spot well. Or someone had picked it well for him.

Seb took a drink of the juice and shoved the bottle into his jacket pocket. He'd better go before someone wondered what he was doing, loitering around the side of the shop. A man leaning against a wall to have a smoke was a lot more normal than a teenager drinking apple juice.

The library was noisy when he entered. An after-school club was in progress and the exuberant reading of The Gruffalo by the pink-haired librarian was having its desired effect.

"Wahhhh!" they all screamed as Mouse spotted The Gruffalo.

Seb skirted the crowd and headed around the corner to the quieter side of the library. He found a free desk and plopped down in the chair. Pulling out his books, he spread them out and began to work. The cheers of the children reverberated through the building. Two more librarians were talking loudly to each other. Seb sighed. He thought libraries were supposed to be quiet places. The homework wasn't exactly easy either, not helped by the fact that he hadn't heard much of what the teachers had said earlier.

Another ecstatic cheer sounded out. He assumed Mouse must have eaten The Gruffalo to have provoked such a reaction.

"Good," he muttered to himself. "Now that The Gruffalo is dead, I'll maybe get some peace." Seb stared at the chemistry textbook and tried to focus. Chemistry was usually over his head, but today it was so far over his head that he needed a space shuttle to reach it. Gradually, the children quietened down and Seb breathed a sigh of relief. He read through the first question.

"Now, kids," the pink-haired librarian said, "we are going to read…" She paused for dramatic effect. "…The Gruffalo's Child!"

The children went wild. Seb groaned and slammed his chemistry book shut and jammed it into his bag. Swinging the bag over his shoulder, he stood up and marched out of the library, past the talkative librarians, past the cheering children, out the door.

"I can't believe The Gruffalo has a child," he muttered grumpily. "I hope Mouse eats him as well." An elderly man, shuffling along with a zimmer frame, turned and gave him an odd look as Seb strode past.

Dad was in his usual place when Seb arrived home. "Hey, Seb!" he called as Seb closed the door behind him.

Seb closed his eyes and took a deep breath. Dealing with Dad was the last thing Seb wanted to do this bothersome day. "Yes?" he called.

"Come here!" Dad demanded.

Seb reluctantly moved to the living room door.

"Do you need some more money?" Dad asked, as he lifted his wallet from the top of the pile of junk on the coffee table.

Seb shrugged. He actually did need money – what he had left wouldn't buy him very much dinner tonight.

"Here you go." Dad reached into his wallet and handed him a few notes. The wallet looked stuffed full. Dad must have got paid for the transfer he made last night.

Seb took the money. "Thanks."

"No bother, Seb. I told you I had plenty of money, didn't I?" He chuckled and took a swig of beer. He seemed to be in high spirits.

Seb turned to go.

"Here, what about getting a Chinese take away tonight?" Dad asked. "Amanda's coming round."

Seb blinked. Dad was asking Seb to join them? He hadn't eaten with his dad since...he couldn't remember when. He wasn't sure why Dad was asking, but still, it had been a long time since he'd had Chinese food. "That's fine with me," he replied, then headed upstairs to try to get to grips with the chemistry homework.

———

Amanda arrived at seven with a large bag of Chinese food. Seb was ravenous. Amanda swept all the magazines and newspapers onto the floor and began to set out the bags and plastic containers onto the bare coffee table. Seb's mouth watered at the delicious aromas. He found a few dusty plates in the cupboard, rinsed three off and grabbed a few forks. He took them to the living room and returned for three glasses.

"I don't think we need those," laughed Amanda. "Your dad is drinking his beer as usual, and I brought cans of coke for us."

Seb took a seat on the armchair. Dad opened one of the plastic containers and tipped half the contents onto a plate, then proceeded to do the same thing with the next one.

"You'd better grab a plate and some food," Amanda said, helping herself to fried rice. "If you don't, your dad will eat the lot."

Seb lifted the nearest container and opened it up. He hadn't a clue what it was, but he took some of the contents, and some rice. Dad had already begun shovelling food into his mouth. Seb took a deep breath. "Um, Dad?"

Dad looked up. Red sauce dribbled down his chin. "What is it? Eat up!" He waved a fork at him and rice sprinkled over the carpet.

"I was going to give thanks for the food."

"Well, hurry up and thank Amanda, and then eat."

"That's not what I meant–"

Dad leaned forward. "You mean *saying grace?*" he bellowed. Rice and chewed meat sprayed from his mouth.

"Alan!" exclaimed Amanda. "That's disgusting!"

"*Not in my house!*" Dad yelled. "I can't believe you're still going on about that nonsense! I thought I'd have got that out of you by now."

Was that the real reason Dad had wanted him to live here?

"Now, eat up, before I shove it down your scrawny throat!"

Seb looked at his plate. The food he'd looked forward to all afternoon suddenly didn't seem so appetising anymore. All the same, he needed to eat. He bowed his head and closed his eyes. No matter what Dad said, he was grateful to God for this meal. As he opened his eyes, he heard the clunk of a plate hitting the top of the coffee table. Dad was struggling to his feet, a look of uncontrolled anger in his eyes.

"Alan! ALAN!" said Amanda. She grabbed his arm and tried to haul him back to his seat on the sofa. He shook her off. She stood up and tried to block his way, but he shoved her aside.

As he began to advance, Seb scrambled to his feet and hurried to the door.

"You wait here, you little Christian coward!" screamed Dad. Seb yanked the door open and turned sharply to climb the stairs.

Dad wouldn't be able to catch him, but in his current state he'd knock the bedroom door down anyway. Should he run outside? His shoes were in his bedroom and he was still holding his plate. In the moment of indecision, Dad reached him and grabbed his arm. He swung Seb around and the contents of the plate spread over the floor. Dad's face was red and his nostrils were dilated. He looked like an angry bull Seb had seen during the summer. Dad narrowed his eyes and pulled his fist back.

Seb closed his eyes and waited for the painful blow.

Chapter Twenty-Four

The blow never came. Instead, a mobile phone ringtone sliced through the charged atmosphere and Dad loosened his grasp of Seb's arm. Seb pulled away and dashed upstairs, still clutching his plate. He slammed his bedroom door shut behind him and leaned against it, breathing heavily. His heart was pounding and he was trembling. Dad in one of his rages was terrifying on any occasion, but this was the angriest he'd ever seen him. And to think that it had only been triggered by Seb giving thanks for his food. Seb frowned and wondered yet again why Dad became so angry when God was mentioned.

A gentle tap sounded at the door and Seb jumped.

"It's me." Amanda.

Seb pushed away from the door and gingerly opened it a tiny crack. The tall redhead was standing with a new plate of food in one hand and a can of coke in the other. She gave Seb a watery smile.

Seb pulled the door open and she entered, perching herself on the bed. "I brought you some food. You might be hungry before tomorrow."

Seb took the plate. His appetite had left him, but Amanda was right – he would be hungry later. He took the fork she offered and sank onto the floor, back pressed against the wall. The food which, a short time before, had had such a tantalising aroma, tasted like cardboard in his mouth.

Amanda crossed her long skinny-jean clad legs and clasped her hands around her knee. She looked as if she was a thousand miles away; her perfectly made-up face looked sad. She looked up and saw Seb watching her. She rearranged her face into a smile. "The honey chilli beef is good, isn't it?"

Seb nodded out of politeness.

Amanda sighed. "Has your dad always been like that?"

Seb washed his mouthful down with a long drink of coke. He set the can beside him on the floor and chased his food around the plate. "Violent?" he finally asked.

Amanda nodded.

"Yes, but when I lived here I wasn't a Christian. Dad hates Christians."

Amanda's brow furrowed. "Why? I used to go to Sunday school when I was little. The Christians I knew were the kindest people in my life."

Seb looked up. Amanda had been to Sunday school? "Do you still go to church?" he asked.

Amanda laughed. "Oh, no! I'm not sure that there is a God,

but I don't want to kill people who disagree!" She stood up and straightened the hem of her top.

"There is a God, Amanda," said Seb. "He loves us and gave His Son to die for our sins."

Amanda laughed, a hard, cynical laugh. "Ah, Seb, I love your innocence, but you don't know about my life. If you did, you wouldn't be telling me that God loves me. If He's really there, He doesn't care."

Seb pushed to his feet and set his plate on the bed. He looked Amanda in the eye. " 'For God so loved the world that He gave His only begotten Son, that whoever–' "

" '–believes in Him should not perish but have everlasting life.' I remember that verse, Seb."

"But it's true, Amanda!"

Amanda shrugged. "That's your opinion." She walked to the door and put her hand on the door handle. She turned back and looked at Seb. "I just came upstairs to tell you that I won't be coming around here anymore. I've known too many men like your dad, and…" Her face crumpled and her eyes filled with tears. "Seb, pray for me." With that, she was gone.

Seb stared at the closed door. He didn't know how long he sat there, praying for Amanda. She was hurting, deeply. Seb was certain that she really did believe in God's existence, but didn't seem to recognise that God's salvation would transform her life and give her hope. He prayed that soon she would accept the wonderful truth of the verse that had been hidden in her heart for so many years.

———

Seb had no intention of venturing downstairs until the morning, so he was alarmed to hear the heavy tread of Dad's footsteps on the stairs. In a panic, Seb threw himself against the closed, locked door and leaned against it. He knew that Dad could burst it open in one shove, but he didn't know what else to do.

Dad shook the door handle. "Seb!"

Seb blinked. Dad didn't sound angry at all. He sounded...jovial? Was this a trick?

"Seb! Come on, son. Open up!" Dad gave the handle a vigorous rattle.

Seb winced. No matter what he did, he wasn't going to win. He'd be better opening the door now while Dad sounded fairly calm. Maybe he could reason with him. He unlocked the door and pressed down on the handle.

Seb stood aside as Dad pushed the door open and strode into the room. He marched over to the window and glanced out into the dimly-lit yard, then turned back. He had a triumphant look on his face and was rubbing his hands together. What was going on? He'd obviously forgotten all about the episode over dinner.

Chapter Twenty-Four

"Guess what?" he boomed.

Seb shrugged, confused. What was making Dad so happy? Had he even realised yet that Amanda had left?

"I'm going on a holiday!" he exclaimed.

A holiday? Seb couldn't remember Dad ever going on a holiday; there had never been enough money. And why now?

"Where?" asked Seb.

"I'm going to Amsterdam." Dad's hand-rubbing reached new levels of vigour.

"Amsterdam?" echoed Seb. "When?"

"This weekend," replied Dad. "I'll be back on Sunday night." He clapped his hands together and rubbed again. "Always wanted to go to Amsterdam," he chortled.

Seb frowned. "Who else is going?"

"No one," Dad replied. "I'm going myself." He grinned. "Oh, I'm going to have a great time." With that, he left the room and trudged back downstairs to the football match on TV.

Seb closed the door and relocked it. Nothing was making sense. He had heard of Amsterdam. He knew there were different reasons why people went to Holland – some went to see the canals, windmills and tulips. It didn't take a lot of effort to work out that that wasn't what Dad wanted to see. But why so soon? And why did he make this decision immediately after he'd almost hit Seb?

Seb froze as the realisation dawned on him. The phone call! Had some of Dad's contacts phoned Dad and told him that he had to visit Amsterdam? Not only would Dad get to spend time in the 'brown cafes' and amongst the dens of iniquity in the city, he would also gain a huge payment for transporting money or drugs! It was a risky venture, nothing like passing a small package to someone outside a filling station. Dad would have to avoid security checks and customs officials, but he was so greedy that the risks and implications of being caught hadn't even seemed to register.

Seb flopped backwards onto the bed. What would he do now? Surely the authorities would catch Dad. Then what? And what if they didn't…?

Seb sat up and lifted his Bible. The red ribbon marker was in the epistle of James, where he had been reading, at chapter four. His eyes scanned the chapter, but his brain didn't take anything in. Until the final verse. Seb reeled as he read the words. 'Therefore, to him who knows to do good and does not do it, to him it is sin.' Would doing good involve notifying the police of his dad's activities? Surely it was none of his business. And, as well as that, he didn't have any proof. Perhaps Dad really had decided to book a spontaneous trip to Amsterdam. It wasn't impossible…

Seb closed the Bible, set it on the bedside table and quickly changed for bed. He flipped off the light and climbed under the quilt. He made himself comfortable and tried to sleep.

…to him it is sin… to him it is sin… to him–

Seb groaned and pulled the quilt around his ears, trying to block out the voice. He couldn't phone the police. What would he say? "Oh, hello! My dad has booked a trip to Amsterdam and I think you should keep an eye on him." Seb snorted sarcastically. Sure, they'd really take him seriously. They might even arrest *him* for wasting police time.

...knows to do good...

Seb threw back the covers and got out of bed. He was never going to be able to sleep with the words of Scripture running through his head, convicting, convincing.

Did God really mean that he should tell on Dad? Why couldn't he just ignore what Dad was up to? It wasn't really affecting Seb.

But it is affecting other people, came a quiet voice.

Seb sighed. His conscience was right. Dad was a link in a long chain which bound people to their addictions and sin, which would ultimately land them in hell. Drugs affected people's minds and bodies, gave rise to other crimes and sins – burglary, violence, immorality and murder, they destroyed homes and families, and even led to death. Dad's intention was likely to bring more drugs to the streets of the towns and cities of Northern Ireland, destroying more lives.

Seb dropped to his knees. How could he ignore what he was certain was going to happen? He had a duty to report it. It was what the law demanded, and it was what God expected. Closing his eyes, he committed the situation to God, asking for courage and for His help.

———

Seb yawned and stretched. Something niggled deep in his mind. What was it? Slowly, the previous evening's events bubbled to the surface. Dad. Amsterdam. A slow sense of dread accompanied the memory. He knew what had to be done. It didn't mean he was looking forward to it, though. What time was it anyway? The sunlight was streaming through his thin curtains. He swung his legs out of bed and reached for his phone, peering at the screen through sleep-blurred eyes. The hand holding the phone stilled. He blinked. Surely not! Did it really read 8:51am?

Springing to his feet, he began to hurriedly change. He was late! There was no time to think about phoning the police. Right now, his priority was getting to school. If he hurried, he might make it for the beginning of Miss Carruthers' physics class.

———

Seb spent the day in a distracted haze. More than once Edward asked what was wrong, but Seb wouldn't say. This was something that he wanted to do with complete anonymity and not even his closest school friend could know what was going on.

When the bell rang to signal the end of the day, Seb bypassed the library and went straight home. He couldn't concentrate on anything else until he had done what he needed to do.

He unlocked the door and pushed it open. Dad wasn't at home. Seb dumped his schoolbag at the bottom of the stairs and went into the kitchen to get a drink of water. As usual, it was a mess. He filled a glass and carried it through to the living room. The magazines and papers were still on the floor where Amanda had put them last night, and the take away cartons were piled up on the coffee table beside a brown envelope. Seb frowned. What was that? He set his glass on the floor and lifted the envelope. It had already been opened. Seb pulled out a stack of pages and unfolded them, flipping through them. Boarding passes for flights to and from Amsterdam. He scanned through them, taking a mental note of the times. Dad was leaving first thing tomorrow morning and arriving back around dinnertime on Sunday evening. Other pages had train times and hotel details, and a final page had a handwritten address. Seb glanced over his shoulder. This information might be useful.

He pulled his phone from his pocket to take photos of the details. He had just entered his pin code when he heard a car pull up outside. He glanced out the window. Dad's car. Quickly, he shoved the papers back into the envelope and threw it on the table. He reached into his schoolbag and pulled out a pen and a pad of paper. He was writing

'Romeo and Juliet' at the top just as Dad opened the front door.

Dad didn't seem to be alarmed by Seb's presence in the living room. "Doing your homework here today?" he asked, as he pulled out a packet of cigarettes and a lighter.

Seb nodded. "The library was too noisy yesterday."

Dad snorted with laughter. "You are unbelievable," he said, shaking his head. "What kind of a son have I got that finds libraries too noisy?" He turned on the TV and increased the volume, giving Seb a wicked look.

Seb looked down at his page, then gathered his books and left the room, Dad's laughter following him up the stairs.

Seb had only pulled his textbooks from his schoolbag when the TV abruptly quietened. He heard Dad's voice quite clearly through the silence.

"Yes, I'm all set… can't wait to get there… oh, I know, I know, I'll be careful, don't you worry… those airport boys won't suspect a thing, picture of innocence, that's me… " A loud guffaw. "… sure, okay, see you Sunday. Bye. Bye. Bye."

Seb took a deep breath. If he had the slightest doubt before that Dad was doing something illegal, he certainly had none now. He shivered. No matter the consequences, he had to go through with this.

In the morning, as soon as Dad left, he would phone the police.

Chapter Twenty-Five

Dad was ready to leave when Seb came downstairs the next morning. A new black cabin case sat at the front door. Dad was shrugging into his favourite dark blue jacket. It looked grubby, stains down the front, and reeked of cigarette smoke. Seb pitied the person who'd have to sit beside him on the plane.

"Well, Seb, I'm ready to go!" Dad exclaimed, reaching down to pick up the case and knocking it over. He seemed a little on edge. Seb wondered if the risk was beginning to sink in.

"Do you have your passport?" Seb asked.

Dad's eyes widened and he clapped his hands to his jacket pockets, then to the back of his jeans, before dropping the case and racing up the stairs. Seb stared after him. He'd never seen Dad move so fast before. Crashes and bangs sounded from upstairs as Dad overturned furniture and tipped out drawers. Seb waited. Soon he heard the thud of Dad's footsteps making their way towards the stairs.

"Good job you said," Dad exclaimed, coming into view. "I'd forgotten all about it."

"I didn't know you had a passport," Seb commented. He'd certainly never seen one before.

"I only got it lately. Bi… ah, someone told me it could come in handy and I'd better get one while I can."

Seb frowned. "While you can?" he echoed. Did Dad have an inkling that he might just end up with a criminal record someday?

Dad's face paled. "Ah, yes, you know, they're tightening up… making it harder… ah… Well. I'd better go. Don't want to miss my flight." He opened the door and left without another word.

Seb rolled his eyes. Dad was so indiscreet that Seb likely wouldn't even need to tip the police off about what Dad was up to. Instead, he was sure to drop himself in it.

But, all the same, now that Seb had made the decision to do the right thing, he needed to go ahead with it.

He picked up his phone and began to search 'reporting crimes'. He soon discovered that he could either phone, or fill out an online form, either to a charity set up for that purpose, or to the police themselves. Reporting it to the charity meant he could remain anonymous. He clicked on the form and began to fill out the questions. The first question was simple – it was asking what the crime was. He ticked the box for 'drug trafficking/supply' and moved on.

Where did it happen? Seb frowned. He could report the package transfer, but primarily he wanted to explain his suspicions about Dad's trip to Amsterdam. The problem was that Dad had only left. He scanned the rest of the questions. They all asked about a crime which had already taken place. How was he going to report a crime which was in the future?

He glanced at his watch. It was almost time to leave for school. Later, he promised himself, he'd phone and report it.

———

Seb sighed with relief as he touched his finger to the red 'end call' icon. The lady on the other end of the phone had been thorough and had asked plenty of questions. He hoped that the information that he had given would now be put to good use.

He pulled his textbooks out of his bag and got to work.

———

Saturday passed slowly. Seb finished not only his homework, but an assignment which wasn't due to be handed in until after half term. He slid the stack of printed sheets carefully into his bag and stood up. What should he do the rest of the day? He was still avoiding Edward's house. Edward and his parents had come to an uneasy truce and Seb didn't want to jeopardise it. He could go and wander around the shops, but he didn't really feel like facing the Saturday crowds. He wished Mrs Thompson was home, but the last he'd heard, she had prolonged her stay in London and wasn't due home for another few weeks.

Seb left the house and locked the door behind him. He had to go somewhere, take his mind off what Dad was doing.

As he wandered down the road, a thought penetrated his mind. Mum. How long had it been since he had spoken to her? He'd texted her regularly, and very occasionally they chatted on the phone, but he was always wary of letting it slip that he was living with Dad. He'd always been able to give a vague answer and change the subject when she asked about Mrs Thompson's friends.

Maybe it was the right time to go and visit, while Dad was away. He pulled out his phone and called her.

———

Mum looked well. Her face had healed up and she was relaxed and smiling. She had changed her hair colour to a darker, more natural shade of blonde, which suited her.

"How are you, Seb?" she said, engulfing him in a hug. "I've missed you!"

Seb winced. He didn't like all that mushy-gushy stuff. He pulled back quickly.

"Okay," he replied as he looked around the small room. It was like what he imagined a room in a nursing home might look like: thin green carpet and plain wooden furniture.

"How are you getting on with Mrs Thompson's friends? I can't believe how kind they are, keeping you for so long. It won't be much longer, though," she continued without waiting for an answer, to Seb's relief. "I've been making plans." Her blue eyes sparkled.

"What kind of plans?" Seb asked.

"Wait and see," she said, smiling.

Seb figured he knew what the plans were. She'd obviously found another house, somewhere safer. Seb couldn't enter into his mum's enthusiasm, for he knew that if he went to live with Mum, Dad would search for him and the same thing would happen again. Mum's only protection was in him living with his dad, but how long would it be before he wanted Mum under his control again, especially when he discovered Amanda wasn't coming back?

He jumped when Mum's hand touched his arm. "What is it, Seb? You don't look excited."

Seb shrugged. "I've a lot on my mind. School…" He vaguely waved a hand in the air.

Mum frowned. "No more trouble with those boys again?"

Seb shook his head. While Tyler and Corey frequently threw scathing glances in his direction, they had barely spoken to him in weeks.

"Are you keeping up with the work?"

Seb nodded. "It's hard, but I'm getting there."

Mum leaned over and looked into his eyes. "So what is it? The new Seb that came home from Cherryhill at the end of the summer has lost his sparkle."

Seb looked down and bit his lip. All of a sudden, the pressures and burdens of the past few weeks assailed him – the difficulties with school and schoolwork, Mum's injuries, being sent to live with strangers who didn't want him, then having to live with Dad with all its associated problems, and now the knowledge that his dad was a drug trafficker. A heavy weight pressed down inside him and he felt unable to take a deep breath.

If he hadn't known any better, he might have thought that he actually wanted to cry.

He was conscious of Mum standing up and reaching for something, then sitting back down opposite him.

"Seb, I don't know what's going on, but there's something bothering you, isn't there?"

Seb reluctantly nodded.

"Listen to this." He heard the rustle of pages turning, then Mum cleared her throat. "Psalm 61. I was reading this just this morning. 'Hear my cry, O God; attend to my prayer. From the end of the earth I will cry to You, when my heart is overwhelmed; lead me to the rock that is higher than I...' "

Overwhelmed. Exactly how Seb was feeling right now. What did it say? *I will cry... lead me to the rock that is higher than I.* Seb certainly needed something outside of himself. Something – or someone – bigger, better, stronger, wiser. He needed the shelter which would withstand and absorb the blows of life. For somehow he knew, deep down, that the waves were increasing in force and power, and if his feet weren't planted firmly on the Rock, he'd be engulfed.

———

BOOM! BOOM! BOOM!

Seb sat bolt upright in bed. What was that?

The noises sounded again. BOOM! BOOM! BOOM!

Seb whipped back the covers and stood up, legs trembling. Who was banging the door so late on Sunday night? Or was it Monday morning? He hadn't heard Dad return from his weekend away. Seb wasn't sure if he was celebrating a successful trip, or whether the tip-off had done its job. Maybe Dad was back. Maybe he had lost his key and needed in. The bangs didn't sound like noises a drunk man made, though.

"Police! Open up!"

The police! Seb raced downstairs. He could see a number of uniformed men through the glass in the door. He unlocked the door and pulled it open.

"Police Service of Northern Ireland," stated the tall, flint-faced police officer. "We need to search this property."

Seb pulled the door wide open and stepped aside while a number of officers and a bright-eyed Springer Spaniel entered. He shut the door behind them and stood uncertainly in the hallway while they dispersed around the house. He figured they must have arrested Dad, but he didn't want to ask, scared of letting slip that he was the one who reported him.

He watched the dog at work in the living room, head down, long brown ears alert, sniffing the sofa, the doors of the cabinet, the windowsill and behind the chairs. She moved to the coffee table and worked her way up and down the length of newspapers and magazines which somehow had got piled back onto it. She abruptly stopped, then worked her way backwards, before planting herself on the ground. Seb marvelled at how the little bundle of energy was able to sit so still. Her handler threw her a ball from his pocket and she relaxed while he began to carefully search through the pile with gloved hands.

Seb's eyes widened as the officer pulled a little package out from the middle of one of the newspapers and unfolded it to reveal a small amount of white crystalline powder. While he'd had his suspicions that Dad wasn't just a transporter and trafficker, he'd never seen him actually using it.

The officer bagged the find and labelled it, and the dog resumed its frantic and joyous sniffing around the house. Despite the seriousness of the situation, Seb couldn't help but smile at the dog. She didn't even seem to realise she was working; it was so much fun for her.

"Found something!" A call rang from upstairs. Apart from one, all the police officers downstairs stomped up the stairs to join their colleague.

"Why don't you come in and sit down?" the young ginger-haired police officer asked Seb from the door of the living room. "You don't have to hang around the door."

Seb slowly walked into the living room, perching himself on the armchair. He wondered what had been found upstairs to cause such an immediate reaction. Probably more drugs. He purposely avoided Dad's bedroom, so he'd no idea what they might find amongst the mess and filth.

"Which room is yours?" One of the officers, a middle-aged lady, had entered the room.

"The small one at the top of the stairs," answered Seb.

"With all the schoolbooks?"

Seb nodded.

"Anyone else ever go into it?"

"I don't think so."

The officer narrowed her eyes at Seb. What was wrong? Why was she asking questions like these?

The remaining officers came down the stairs and entered the room. One was holding a long object in his hands, encased in a clear evidence bag. "This was found in your room, at the back of the shelf in your wardrobe."

Seb looked up and gaped in horror.

Resting in the officer's hands was a gun.

Chapter Twenty-Six

Seb sat in the back of the police car, dejected and confused. What on earth had the gun been doing there? That was the first he'd ever known about it. Obviously Dad had hidden it, but no amount of trying to protest his innocence was making any impact on the police officers. He'd groaned when he'd seen the crowd that had gathered in the early morning light as he was escorted out of the house, and his heart sank as he spotted Edith at the front, flabby arms crossed over a large brown apron, a disapproving frown on her face. Seb caught her eye as he scanned the crowd and she shook her head with disgust. Seb's breath had caught in his throat. *She actually believes I've done something wrong*, he thought, aghast. Maybe Rebekah was right – trouble really did follow him around.

What a mess! He'd thought he was doing the right thing, going back to live with Dad. Why had he felt that keeping Mum safe was his responsibility? Why hadn't he told Uncle Matt what had happened? In fact, why hadn't he prayed about any of the decisions he'd made? The police car turned out the end of the street onto the main road.

Seb felt like such a failure. He'd done what he'd planned never to do again. He had let God down.

———

The police station was full of noise and bustle. Seb had been ushered into a small room and left by himself as they tried to contact his mum. She would be alarmed and devastated, not only because he was in a police station awaiting questioning, but by the fact that he'd been living with Dad and hadn't even told her. The door opened and a lady set down a cup of tea and a biscuit before him on the desk, then left. He wasn't hungry, but he absentmindedly nibbled the biscuit. He felt as if he was in a different world.

As Seb pondered his predicament, he began to pray. Haltingly at first, confessing his sin, his lack of trust, how he had acted by himself, often refusing to listen for God's voice. As he prayed, the words of his favourite verse came into his mind. 'The blood of Jesus Christ His Son cleanses us from all sin.' All sin. Seb was forgiven. 'If we confess our sins, He is faithful and just to forgive us our sins and to cleanse us from all unrighteousness.' Forgiven and cleansed. Seb took a deep breath and smiled. Communion was restored between him and his heavenly Father.

The door creaked open and a blonde-haired police officer entered. She took a seat behind the desk. "We haven't been able to contact your mum. Is there another adult you know who you'd like to be present? I need to ask you some questions."

Seb slowly shook his head. Mrs Thompson was in London, and, while he hadn't committed any crimes, he felt awkward about asking anyone he'd met at church to be present while the police officer questioned him.

"That's okay," the officer answered. "We can find a volunteer." She left the room and returned a short while later with a tall, gangly, grey-haired man with large, gold-rimmed spectacles, whom she introduced as Niall.

The police officer directed Niall to a chair in the corner and took a seat behind the desk. "Okay, we're ready to begin. Firstly, I need to read you this caution." She cleared her throat. "You do not have to say anything. But it may harm your defence if you do not mention when questioned something which you later rely on in court. Anything you do say may be given in evidence."

Seb nodded. He felt calm, at peace. He had done nothing wrong in the eyes of the law. He had nothing to be afraid of.

A few hours later, the officer smiled at Seb. "You are free to go," she told him. "We have found nothing that connects you to the weapon found on the premises."

Seb stood up, relieved, a prayer of thanksgiving bursting from his heart. He had told them everything that he knew. "What about Dad?" he asked.

The officer hesitated. "Sit down," she said. "I can tell you that a man was arrested at Amsterdam Schiphol airport last night. He was trying to board a flight bound for Belfast, with a significant quantity of cocaine. He is to be extradited to face charges here in the UK."

Seb nodded solemnly. While it was what he had expected to hear, he still felt sorry for Dad.

"Do you have anyone you can go and live with? Your mum?"

"She's…" Seb paused. Did they know she was in a shelter? Maybe it would be best not to go into that story without her permission. He shook his head instead. "I can stay with friends." But which friends?

As he left the police station, he breathed a sigh of relief. He had been cleared of all charges. It felt good. More than good, actually.

He whistled as he walked. It was a long way home, but he had plenty of time. There was no point in going to school today – by the time he went home for his books and walked to school, it would be over. Maybe he should text Edward later and ask what they had done that day.

———

Seb pulled the quilt around his shoulders. He hoped the police wouldn't check to see if he had moved elsewhere. Mum had said it wouldn't be long until she got her new house sorted, and when she did, he would move there. Wherever it was, he was looking forward to living in a safe, calm, clean, tidy house again and eating proper meals. He wasn't looking forward to explaining to Mum why he hadn't told her he'd been living with Dad. Maybe she wouldn't be too annoyed once she found out Dad was behind bars. Would Seb have discovered that Dad was a criminal if had he not been living here? He shrugged. Unlikely, but he didn't really know.

He burrowed beneath the quilt and drifted off to sleep...

———

Bang, bang, bang, bang!

Uncle Matt hammered a nail into the wall of the shed and reached for another.

Bang, bang, bang, bang!

The sound reverberated around the large shed. Jess and Glen spun in tight circles, tails between their legs, terrified of the sound. Seb covered his ears. It was much louder than hammering nails should sound. What was Uncle Matt doing anyway?

Bang, bang, bang, bang!

Seb walked closer and reached out to grab the hammer and stop the awful pounding. He clasped the hammer. It was wrenched from his grasp. Uncle Matt turned around and Seb screamed. It wasn't Uncle Matt at all! The face was that of a monster – huge, red eyes, bared, pointy teeth and flared nostrils. Seb let go of the hammer and struggled away. Something was impeding his progress, tangling him up when he tried to take a step. With all his might, he wrenched himself free...

————

Seb sat bolt upright, breathing heavily. A nightmare. That was all. The scary images were already beginning to recede, but the fear was taking a lot longer to dissipate. He breathed deeply. In. Out. In. Out.

Bang, bang, bang, bang!

Seb froze. There was that noise again! It wasn't in his dream after all. His heart rate ramped up a notch and he broke out in a cold sweat. Who was here, banging his door in the middle of the night? Was it someone who knew he was here alone? Or was it the police, back to check if he was staying here by himself? They would identify themselves, though, wouldn't they? Whoever was banging wasn't saying anything.

Bang, bang, bang, bang!

Seb wished they would just go away and leave him in peace, but that didn't seem likely. Maybe he should check who it was.

He tiptoed out of his room and into Dad's room at the front of the house. Maybe he could peek out the window to see who was below. He picked his way carefully through the piles of rubbish, clothes and other odds and ends, wincing when he stood on the prongs of a plug for a mobile phone charger.

He reached the window and gingerly peered out. He couldn't see who was there; they were evidently right below the overhang which served as a porch roof. The rest of the street was silent and still, no strange cars parked at the kerb.

The banging sounded again, more desperately this time. Seb figured there couldn't be any more than one person, or maybe two small people out there – the overhang couldn't shield any more than that. He decided to go down.

He tiptoed down the stairs. He could hear his heart racing. The streetlights shone through the glass door panel, but he couldn't see anyone there. Maybe whoever it was had left.

He turned the key in the lock and pressed down on the handle. Before he could pull the door open, it was pushed from the outside. Seb jumped hurriedly back before it rammed against his face. A slight form bolted into the hallway and slammed the door shut.

Seb gaped, astonished.

"Zoe?"

The girl pushed her hood back and her dark hair spilled over her shoulders. She was out of breath and wide-eyed. "I thought you were never going to come to the door," she said.

"I was sleeping," Seb replied. "And I don't tend to open the door to strangers in the middle of the night."

"I'm not a stranger!" exclaimed Zoe.

"I know that! But how was I to know it wasn't a red-eyed monster at the door?"

Zoe frowned. "A monster?"

"Never mind. So why are you here? What time is it anyway?"

"It's three o'clock or something like that. Or maybe four, I don't know. I was standing out there for ages."

"So you said. I'm sorry I wasn't waiting up for you to drop by," said Seb sarcastically.

"Ha-ha. Funny!" Zoe rolled her eyes. "I just thought I'd better warn you."

"Warn me?"

"I heard you had a trip to the police station earlier."

"How did you know that?"

"Someone saw you getting into a police car. It was all around school."

Seb grimaced. He could just imagine what was said. *And he calls himself a Christian!*

"I thought you'd better know that Uncle Nigel was arrested this afternoon."

Uncle Nigel. Dad's drugs contact. Seb smiled wryly. The police hadn't wasted any time lifting him after Seb had told them about the handover at the filling station.

"So it was you who gave them the tip-off?" Zoe looked intensely at Seb.

"I'm sorry, Zoe, I know he's your favourite uncle, but the less drugs that are on the streets the better."

"I know that. But you don't know what sort of people you're dealing with. Your dad and Nigel are small players in a bigger game. The whole scene is run by a paramilitary organisation and they don't appreciate people who interfere. My dad is high up in the organisation so I grew up in these circles. You've no idea what those people are involved in and are capable of."

Seb shrugged. He was perfectly aware of the paramilitaries and their activities these days – extortion and blackmail, as well as drugs. He had grown up and went to school in this area of Belfast, after all.

"So you think there'll be some form of retribution? How would they know for sure it was me anyway?"

"Seb," sighed Zoe. "It's so obvious. You get picked up by the police, then Uncle Nigel is arrested almost immediately. Who else would it be?"

"Maybe Dad dropped his name."

"Maybe. But whether it's you or him, they don't care. They can't target your dad right now. Anyway, I overheard a conversation–" She stopped abruptly and listened. A car driving along the street slowed. Her eyes widened.

"Quick," she yelled as she dashed towards the kitchen. "Run!"

Seb had barely turned away when he heard the smashing of glass, coupled with an explosion. He ducked and threw his arm over his head as a bright flash filled his sight. The car revved and sped away, tyres screeching as it turned the corner.

What had just happened?

Seb spun around.

He looked towards the living room and froze in horror.

Chapter Twenty-Seven

Flames were spreading and taking hold faster than Seb could have imagined. They leaped high, lapping the walls. Smoke was being produced at an alarming rate and was already beginning to choke him. He glanced around for Zoe, thinking she was behind him, but she wasn't there. There wasn't a moment to lose.

"Zoe!" he called frantically, making his way to the kitchen. He could hardly see where he was going; smoke was obliterating the orange light from the streetlights. He rounded the corner into the kitchen. Where was she?

"Zoe!" he called again.

"I'm here," came a weak, trembling voice from the corner of the room.

"Zoe, get out! Quickly! The house is on fire." He reached down and pulled her arm. She stood, legs shaking.

"Put your sleeve over your nose," he told her, doing the same. "We need to get out."

He grabbed her arm with his other hand and crouched down. The smoke was billowing thickly around the hallway. Where was the door?

Feeling around the walls, they made their way along. Every second, the smoke grew thicker and hotter. Seb dropped to his knees and tugged Zoe's arm until she dropped to the floor as well. "Hold on to my arm."

They crawled forwards, eyes streaming, trying not to breath the dense smoke. The front door had never seemed so far away. Finally, they could go no further. Eyes stinging, Seb could see nothing but thick blackness. He was becoming dizzy and disorientated.

He turned around. Putting a hand on Zoe's arm, he hauled her after him. They needed to get out the back door. He retraced his path, hand along the wall. Fridge, kitchen cupboards, turn the corner, more cupboards... the door. Seb breathed a sigh of relief and reached up to open it. Locked! He fumbled around to turn the key. It was gone!

The smoke was filling the house. Thick, black, acrid, choking. They wouldn't survive long in this. They needed out. Now.

"Stay low, Zoe. Don't move."

Seb clambered onto the draining board. The smoke was thicker up here, but the kitchen window was their only means of escape. He fumbled on the bench and grabbed the first thing he could find. A heavy wooden worktop saver. He held his breath and smashed it into the glass with all his might. The window shattered, leaving a huge hole in the centre. He revelled in the burst of fresh air.

Working quickly, Seb trimmed the jagged edges.

"Zoe! Come on, let's get out."

There was no response. He leaped off the bench and pulled her arm. It was a dead weight. Seb panicked. Had she been overcome by the smoke?

"God! Help!" he cried hoarsely, as he tried to lift her. She was floppy in his arms and he was feeling weak. "Help! I can't do this!"

With all his might, he managed to lift and shove her limp frame onto the bench. Climbing up beside her, he made his way through the opening and pulled Zoe through behind him.

Zoe fell in a heap outside the kitchen window. At least they were outside, but the fire was taking hold. And what about the neighbours?

Using strength he didn't know he possessed, he pulled Zoe's limp frame as far from the house as he could. He hoped it was far enough away. The small back yards were totally enclosed; garden walls of the neighbours at each side and the tall fence separating the houses from the railway at the back. They might be out of the house, but they were trapped.

Seb slumped against the fence, totally exhausted. "God, give me strength," he prayed in a whisper. He could hear the neighbours' pit bull terrier beginning to bark. Seb hoped he would alert his owners. He stood up and aimed his voice towards the house at the other side.

"Fire! Get out!" he called, but his voice came out as a hoarse croak. Lights came on in the house to his right, the owners obviously awakened by the dog. Seb prayed they had enough time to get out safely. The house to his left lay still and silent.

He looked desperately around for a way to climb the fence. The yard was full of rubbish, but there was nothing that he could use to stand on. Grabbing a beer can, he aimed it at the upstairs window, but it fell short. Seb went closer, but the heat from the house was growing in intensity, flames now billowing from kitchen window.

Searching the ground for anything, he found a broken brick. Taking aim, he took a breath and launched it, with all his might, at the window of the house. It bounced against the window frame. Seb sank onto the ground, utterly spent. How would he ever alert his neighbours to their danger?

Over the roar and crackle of the flames, he heard a shout. Seb lifted his head in time to see the horrified face of the lady next door pulling back inside her window. He breathed a sigh of relief. Now she could get out before the fire spread.

He could hear sirens approaching. Help was near, as long as they could survive a little longer, so close to the inferno. Sparks were leaping from the house onto the ground nearby. He hoped they would soon discover where they were. Zoe needed help, and soon.

He reached for Zoe's wrist. Was there a pulse? They had done a little first aid at school, but that had been a few years ago and he had spent the lesson laughing with his friends at the dummy used for resuscitation practice.

Seb began to panic. He couldn't find a pulse, and the flames were becoming hotter and hotter. The metal fence behind was reflecting the heat back at them. He struggled to stay calm, to stay alert. But it was too much. Black spots danced before his eyes and he felt his body slump to the ground. Then nothing.

———

"Stay still. Don't move." The voice was soft, but commanded obedience. Seb blinked and lifted his hand. It felt heavy. He let it drop back down. He opened his eyes a fraction, only to close them again. Wherever he was, it was too bright.

"How do you feel?" The voice spoke again.

Seb tried to shrug, then froze. His whole body was sore and stinging, like a really bad sunburn.

"Wh–" He stopped and licked his lips. They were swollen and cracked. He tried again. "Where am I?" he asked, his voice hoarse.

"You're in hospital, Seb." Mum! He turned his head in her direction and tried again to open his eyes. This time, he managed to focus on her. She looked pale, dark circles under her eyes, a worried look on her face.

Hospital. Seb pondered the word. What had happened to land him in hospital?

Gradually, then faster and faster, the memories began to flood back. Zoe. Fire. Smoke. Flames. Trapped. Kitchen window. Broken. Back yard. Zoe again. Neighbours.

"Zoe?" he asked.

"She's fine," replied Mum. "She's in hospital too, but, thank God, she's going to be okay. You both are."

Seb gave a little nod. He was exhausted. The rest of the details could wait.

———

Seb's Bible rested open on the bed in front of him. He tried to concentrate on the words, but his mind kept wandering. So much had happened in a very short space of time. Mum had told him she'd been horrified when she'd found out where he'd been living and what he'd been doing. She still hadn't told him where they would be moving. All she would tell him was that it would be soon. Maybe even by the time he got out of hospital.

He heard approaching footsteps and looked up. A smile broke across his face.

"Well, Seb," said Uncle Matt, shaking his head. "What have you got yourself into this time?" He smiled.

Seb smiled back.

"How are you doing?" asked Aunt Karen, looking concernedly at his bandaged hands.

"Okay," he replied. "Nothing serious. It'll heal."

"That's good," said Lavinia. "Half term is really close and you said you'd come to the farm at half term."

Aunt Karen laughed. "Lavinia, dear, we'll wait and see how Seb feels first."

Uncle Matt pulled chairs from the table in the centre of the room to the edge of Seb's bed. They sat down.

"Seb," he began, looking serious, "why didn't you tell me that you were living with your dad?"

Seb looked down and bit his cracked lip. "I'm really sorry, Uncle Matt," he replied. "It's a long story."

"So your mum said," interjected Aunt Karen. "She told us about having to go into a shelter." Aunt Karen tried to hide her hurt at having been kept in the dark.

Seb adjusted the blanket covering his legs. "It was one thing after another. Dad saw me one day and said that if I didn't come to live with him, he would find Mum and hurt her. I was sure he would kill her. But then things got even more complicated when I found out he was involved in the drugs trade. It got to the stage that I couldn't tell you because I'd hidden so much." He looked up. Matt and Karen were watching him. They looked sad, but they weren't angry. "I'm really sorry."

Aunt Karen reached out a hand and rubbed his upper arm. "And we forgive you," she said, smiling.

Uncle Matt nodded. "It was a difficult situation for you, Seb. I'm glad you're okay."

"And that your mum got saved!" Aunt Karen's face lit up. "You've no idea how much I've prayed for her."

"I still can't believe all those things that you did. I mean, you were at the police station! I've never even been inside a police station!" Lavinia exclaimed.

Uncle Matt chuckled. "And just make sure you keep it that way," he told his daughter.

They chatted until the bell rang to signal the end of visiting hours. When Uncle Matt, Aunt Karen and Lavinia left, Seb rested his head back against the clean white pillow. It felt so good to be safe, to have all the secrets out in the open, and to be no longer carrying the weight of deception around.

He closed his eyes and began to thank God for all the blessings and good things he'd experienced over the past few days.

Chapter Twenty-Eight

Seb walked slowly past the nurses' station. Mum walked beside him, carrying a white plastic bag with his newly acquired belongings.

"All the best, Seb!" said one of the nurses.

"Thank you," called Seb, as he pressed the button to open the automatic door. It seemed strange to be dressed in normal clothes again. He still felt a bit weak, but he was glad to be going home.

Well, not exactly home. Mrs Thompson's house. Once their former landlord had heard why they'd had to leave, he was happy to cancel the contract. Mum still hadn't told Seb where their new house was, and he was getting impatient.

"Wait here," Mum told Seb when they reached the large entrance area. "I'll phone for a taxi."

The taxi arrived and Mum held the door open for Seb. She slid in beside him and shut the door. They set off through the familiar streets of the city.

"Mrs Thompson was so kind to let us stay at her house for a few nights," Mum said. "Of course, I had to tell her what had happened. She wasn't very happy with Jimmy and Edith, sending you off to

Alan, but they wouldn't have known what he was really like. I know how good he can be at pretending to be someone he's not."

"Is she back from London yet?"

Mum shook her head. "Not yet. Although when she heard what had happened, she wanted to take the first plane home to look after us both! It took quite a bit of convincing to get her to stay on in London."

Seb laughed. "I hope our new house is close enough to Mrs Thompson so that we can visit her often. I miss her baking!"

"Trust you, Seb! You still think of nothing but your stomach!"

"Well, I hope it's close enough that I can go with her to the Bible study and the prayer meeting. I really missed going when I was living with Dad."

"You didn't go?"

"I found a church near Dad's house and went there a few times. It was good, but not like the one where Mrs Thompson goes." He laughed softly. "There are some very strange places out there." He chuckled again. "Breakfast Breeze-Through."

"Breakfast what?" asked Mum.

The taxi rounded the corner into Mrs Thompson's street. "I'll tell you all about that another time," replied Seb.

———

The doorbell rang and Mum went to the door. Seb was catching up on homework at the kitchen table. Edward had been around earlier in the day with the work Seb had missed. Mum had been very impressed with the young Malaysian fellow and was delighted that he was saved.

Seb heard Mum talking to someone. "Come in. He'll be pleased to see you."

Seb looked up as the person entered the room. "Zoe!" he exclaimed. He hadn't seen her since the night of the fire, a week ago. Zoe perched on the edge of the sofa and Seb took Mrs Thompson's cosy seat. Zoe looked awkward and nervously played with a strand of hair.

"How are you doing?" Seb asked.

"Okay," she said. "I feel a whole lot better." She looked down, then back at Seb. "You saved my life, you know? If you hadn't dragged me out when you did, I'd be dead."

Seb raised his eyebrows. Had he still been in bed when the petrol bomb was thrown through the living room window, it was quite possible he'd never have got out alive. "You saved my life!" he exclaimed. "If you hadn't come to warn me... How did you know anyway?"

Zoe sighed. "It seems so long ago. Uncle Nigel was picked up, and that evening my brother and a couple of his friends were at our house. I was doing my homework in the kitchen and I overheard them saying something about dropping a present off at 'that tout's house'. I didn't know what sort of a present, but I knew it wasn't going to be a box of sweets!"

Seb chuckled drily. "It certainly wasn't! But thank you for coming anyway."

Zoe gave a half-hearted smile. "I wanted to do something right for once. You've been so courageous at school and everything and I'm not."

Seb looked at Zoe. "What do you mean? Why do you want to be courageous?"

Zoe looked down and picked at the pink polish on her fingernails. "I'm a Christian, like you."

Seb looked up, astonished. "You are?" he exclaimed.

Zoe winced. "I know that's a really big shock. I got saved at Sunday school when I was ten, but I've always been too scared to tell anyone, because I knew what they would say."

Seb smiled. It was making sense. He had detected something different about Zoe, but he'd assumed that she was more open to Christianity and the gospel message because she'd been treated well at Sunday school.

"I've decided I don't want to be like that anymore," she said, sitting straight and squaring her shoulders. "I've been wrong. I want to stand up for Jesus now."

Seb's smile erupted into a grin. "That's wonderful news, Zoe. It won't be easy, but it pleases God, and that's all that really counts."

After Zoe left, he went back to his schoolwork, but his mind drifted back over the past few weeks. They'd been tough, and he had failed often, but he could see God's hand, using him as a witness to others. Edward, Zoe, the rest of his schoolmates, Mrs Jones and Mr Symons, his mum, even Amanda. Some accepted the message, some rejected it, but once again, God's Word flooded his mind. *I will never leave you nor forsake you.* And He hadn't. God never lets any of His children down.

Epilogue

"Wake up, Seb!" Mum called as she banged his door. "Today's the big day!"

Seb yawned and stretched. He felt like rolling over and going back to sleep. He had been late to bed last night. Mum had invited Edward's family for dinner and they had talked for a long time, about the Bible, about what happens after death, and other things. Seb smiled as he recalled one comment made by Annie, Edward's mum.

"I always believed that becoming a Christian was a very bad thing," she'd said. "But instead, Edward is a better son than ever. It has changed him in a way that Buddhism can't do."

Seb prayed that soon Edward's whole family would be saved.

"Seb," Mum's voice called from downstairs. "Are you up yet?"

"Almost!" Seb called as he sprang out of bed.

Mum had breakfast ready when he came downstairs. "Hurry, eat up! The removal man will be here in half an hour." Mum turned to go back to the kitchen, but not before Seb saw her mouth twitch in a suppressed grin.

There wasn't going to be much of his stuff to move, thought Seb wryly. All his possessions were lost in the fire. Mum had had to buy him new clothes. He was glad he'd lent her his Bible before she left for the shelter – it was the one that Uncle Matt and Aunt Karen had given him last summer. But everything else was lost.

They had found out that Dad was in prison, awaiting trial. No one was willing to post bail for him and Mum had finally reported him for domestic violence. They had also discovered that Dad had confessed to planting the gun in Seb's wardrobe. Seb had realised that that had been one of the reasons why Dad had wanted him back living with him again; not only had he wanted to control their lives, he'd needed someone to be a scapegoat if things went wrong. Seb felt sorry for Dad. Mum had found a new house and things were looking up, but Dad's life was in a greater mess than ever before.

He needed Christ. Maybe Seb could visit him in prison someday and try to share the good news of the gospel. He prayed that the recent happenings would break Dad down, show him that life without Christ is meaningless and empty.

"Come on, Seb. You're daydreaming!" Mum appeared from the kitchen. "Take your plates in there and get them washed, then go upstairs and gather the rest of your belongings. Strip the bed and bring the bedclothes down here. We don't have time to run a wash, but we'll take them with us and wash them at our new house."

Seb jumped to attention.

———

The doorbell rang. "That'll likely be the removal man," called Seb.

"You get the door," Mum shouted from upstairs.

Seb pulled the door open. His mouth dropped open, then he broke into a grin. "Uncle Matt!" He glanced past his uncle. The jeep was sitting with a trailer attached to the back. "You're the removal man?"

Uncle Matt chuckled. "I am indeed."

They loaded the bags and boxes into the trailer and locked the door. Mum left the key with Herbert, the neighbour who had been looking after Mrs Thompson's cat and plants, and clambered into the jeep. She turned around to smile at Seb.

Seb looked in amazement. Mum actually looked ten years younger! The worry lines had almost gone and she looked bright-eyed and healthy.

"Let's go!"

Uncle Matt started the jeep and they left the street. Seb glanced back. He'd mostly been happy here. They pulled onto the main road. Seb wondered where they were going. Mum hadn't said anything about changing schools, so he figured it was in the same area of Belfast. He hoped it wouldn't be anywhere near Dad's house, not that there was much of a house there anymore.

The traffic thickened as they drove and commercial properties appeared. Seb frowned. It was going to be really far to walk to school. They stopped at traffic lights and Seb caught Uncle Matt's eye in the rear view mirror. Uncle Matt grinned.

A sudden thought crossed Seb's mind. Had Mum finally decided…?

The lights changed to green and Uncle Matt sped forwards, taking the slip road to join the dual carriageway. Could it be…? Seb felt his hopes rise, then tried to quell them.

He waited, watching as the dual carriageway changed to a motorway and Uncle Matt increased his speed.

"Are we leaving the city?" Seb asked casually.

Mum giggled. "Wait and see!"

Seb grinned. They *were* leaving Belfast. Before last summer, he couldn't have imagined living anywhere else, but now it looked as if his dreams of living nearer Cherryhill Farm were coming true.

———

They pulled up in front of a small bungalow in a quiet development.

"Here we are, Seb. Home!" Mum turned and smiled at him.

Seb leaped out of the car. It wasn't in the middle of the country, but behind the fence at the back of the house were green fields with sheep grazing. "Oh, wow!"

Mum laughed. "Wait until you see inside."

She walked up the garden path and pushed open the door. Seb followed her. She turned right into a bright, airy living room.

"SURPRISE!" Aunt Karen, Lavinia, Martha, Caleb and Rebekah shouted. A huge 'Welcome' banner hung over the fireplace and balloons festooned every corner of the room. Everyone began to talk at once.

"You're going to go to our school!" Lavinia said excitedly.

Seb blinked. "Am I?"

Lavinia and Rebekah looked at each other and giggled. Mum put her hand on Seb's shoulder. "Yes, I have it all arranged. You begin the Monday after half term."

Seb smiled. Changing schools was always daunting, but Lavinia and Rebekah would be there. He'd miss Edward and Zoe, of course, but he was glad they'd have each other. Maybe they could come for a visit sometime.

"Now, come and see the rest of the house," Aunt Karen said, as she led him through to the kitchen, then showed him the bathroom and a spacious bedroom at the back of the house.

Seb felt a tug on his trouser leg. "I thought you'd like to watch the sheep." Martha looked up at him, blue eyes bright.

Seb bent down and picked up his little cousin. "Did you pick this room for me?"

She nodded.

Seb smiled. "Good choice, Martha," he said. "This is the nicest room."

Martha beamed.

————

After everyone had gone home, Mum and Seb sat in their new living room with mugs of tea and a plate of cookies that Karen had brought.

"So you like the house?" Mum asked.

"Of course I do! This is amazing!" exclaimed Seb.

"I'm glad. I'm sorry it's not in the country. I thought about it, but because I don't drive and there's very little public transport, it just wasn't going to work. At least we are at the side of town nearest Matt and Karen's. You can walk to school, and I can walk to work."

"You have a new job?"

"Yes, at one of the nursing homes. I start there on Monday. You'll be able to spend time at Matt and Karen's when I have to work late or at weekends."

Seb smiled. His mind drifted back over the past few weeks – the times when he had felt out of control, when he had let God down, when he had felt so alone and miserable. In all his wildest dreams, he never imagined that he would be here, living in a comfortable bungalow, his aunt, uncle and cousins a few miles down the road, and even with sheep grazing across the fence! His heart almost felt like exploding, it was so full of gratitude.

"What are you thinking?" Mum's words broke his reverie.

"I'm just thinking how wonderful God is."

Mum nodded. "He really is, isn't He?" She smiled. "I learned a psalm when I was a little girl. Psalm 107." She cleared her throat.

"Oh, give thanks to the Lord, for He is good! For His mercy endures forever. Let the redeemed of the Lord say so, whom He has redeemed from the hand of the enemy, and gathered out of the lands, from the east and from the west, from the north and from the south. They wandered in the wilderness in a desolate way; they found no city to dwell in. Hungry and thirsty, their soul fainted in them. Then they cried out to the Lord in their trouble, and He delivered them out of their distresses. And He led them forth by the right way, that they might go to a city for a dwelling place. Oh, that men would give thanks to the Lord for His goodness, and for His wonderful works to the children of men! For He satisfies the longing soul, and fills the hungry soul with goodness."

———

Seb climbed under the clean sheets and made himself comfortable. The room was dark, no glare from streetlights and only the occasional car could be heard. A sheep bleated from the field. The psalm that Mum had quoted rang through his mind. *They cried out to the Lord in their trouble, and He delivered them out of their distresses...* God had certainly done that! He had delivered him when Tyler's brother had threatened him, when Dad had almost hit him, when they'd been trapped by the flames. Seb had cried, and God had delivered.

Seb pulled the covers tighter around his chin and yawned. He tried to remember what life had been like before he knew Christ. Empty, purposeless. Seb was glad those days were over. That, no matter what, he was saved, ready for heaven, with a purpose and a goal.

His eyes drifted shut.

He satisfies the longing soul...

Malaysian Customs

Malaysia, a tropical country in south-east Asia, is home to approximately 30 million people, of whom around a quarter are of Chinese ethnicity. This large people group are proud of their Chinese ancestry and continue to hold and practise many Chinese traditions of their culture. Some of these traditions have appeared in the story, such as removing shoes when entering the house, the respect given to older people and the various practices of Buddhism, the most common religion amongst the Malaysian Chinese.

Another tradition alluded to is that of a mealtime ritual, where, in many Malaysian Chinese homes, the younger members of the family will invite the older family members to eat, as Joseph and Edward do in the story.

An important custom that we find in the book and which requires some explanation is the giving of traditional Chinese names. Unlike our western culture, a Chinese name will have the surname first, followed by first names, which are made up of a family middle name and a personal name. The middle name will be the same one which is given to all boys of that generation in the paternal family. Girls may also have a middle family name for their generation.

Seb's friend Edward introduces himself as Edward Lim Chee Meng. Edward's parents, as is quite common in Malaysia, have given each of their children a western name before the surname. *Lim* is his surname, *Chee* is the generational family name, and *Meng* is his other first name. If his parents hadn't given him the western name of Edward, Seb would have called him *Chee Meng*. Edward's brother's full name is Joseph Lim Chee Hua – *Joseph* being his western name; *Lim*, his surname; *Chee*, the generational family name and *Hua* as his other first name. Edward's father doesn't have a western name, and so his full name is Lim Yoon Seng. As before, his surname is *Lim*, and his first names are *Yoon Seng*. However, first names are usually quite personal, and thus it is a mark of respect to call older people 'uncle' and 'aunt', rather than by their Chinese first names.

Malaysia is a fascinating country, with wonderful food and friendly people, and I hope you've enjoyed the little insight into another culture.

Further Reading

When preparing to write a book of this nature, I invariably find and collect much more material than is possible to include without turning a novel into a full-blown apologetics publication. Because of this, I feel it necessary, for anyone who wishes to read more on the topics addressed, to list helpful resources. Some of these resources are very detailed. They do an excellent job of not only refusing to shy away from arguments proposed by prominent neo-atheists today, but they also dig deep into scientific and philosophical matters to show the folly of atheism. For those of us whose minds can become overwhelmed with high levels of intellectualism, other excellent resources are included below which point out the evidence for a Creator and obvious problems with some of the atheists' arguments in an easily-read format. I'd encourage any young person, especially those who are doubting the existence of God, to locate and read more on the topic. Intelligent Christians are very much alive and well, contrary to what the atheists would have you believe. Ask questions and dig deep. Don't let yourself be steamrollered by those who are vehemently opposed to the existence of God, but take a good, honest look at the evidence for yourself.

Burgess, S. *Creation Points. In God's Image – The divine origin of humans.* Day One Publications, 2008.

Cargill, Robert W. *Creation's Story.* John Ritchie Ltd, 2008.

Hodge, B, Mitchell, T and Ham, K. *Answers Book 4 Teens Vol 1.* Master Books, 2011.

Hodge, B, Mitchell, T and Ham, K. *Answers Book 4 Teens Vol 2.* Master Books, 2012.

Lennox, John C. *God's Undertaker* – Has Science Buried God? Lion, 2007.

Randall, David J (Ed). *Why I Am Not An Atheist.* Christian Focus Publications, 2013.

Strobel, L. *The Case for Christ.* Zondervan, 1998.

Zacharias, R, Geisler, N (Ed). *Who Made God? And Answers to Over 100 Other Tough Questions of Faith.* Zondervan, 2003.

The website, *answersingenesis.org*, also contains useful and interesting information.

NB. While these resources can be very helpful, please bear in mind that I do not personally endorse everything that is suggested and taught in some of these publications.

Scripture References